The Shaman
&
His Daughter

The Shaman & His Daughter

A Journey with Two Spiritual Warriors

by
Gregory Drambour

SB
Sacred Bear Press

Published by Sacred Bear Press

Copyright © 2017 Gregory Drambour

All rights reserved. No part of this book may be reproduced or transmitted in any form or by any means, electronic or mechanical, including photocopying, recording or by any information storage and retrieval system, without the written permission from the author, except for the inclusion of brief quotations in a review.

This is a work of fiction. Any resemblance to actual persons, living or dead, or actual events is purely coincidental.

FIRST EDITION
ISBN-13: 978-1973836599
ISBN-10: 1973836599

Cover Photograph: Serendipity © 2015
Used with permission of Michael Irvine.
Silhouette Illustration: My Daddy, used with permission of iStock.
Design: Anugito ten Voorde, Artline Graphics.

For my Angel-Girl

&

For A.M.B.

Table of Contents

Chapter One: Fairy-People	1
Chapter Two: Visiting	9
Chapter Three: The Big Boo-Boo	15
Chapter Four: Three Leaves	21
Chapter Five: Safeway and The Bears	37
Chapter Six: Sparkly Mind	43
Chapter Seven: St. Jude	53
Chapter Eight: The Deer-People	59
Chapter Nine: Faith	65
Chapter Ten: Butterflies	81
Chapter Eleven: Looking for Led Zeppelin	95
Chapter Twelve: The Meeting	101
Chapter Thirteen: Golden-Bear	111
Chapter Fourteen: Fred	131
Chapter Fifteen: The Monsters!	139
Chapter Sixteen: The Choice	147
Chapter Seventeen: Dinosaurs	159
Chapter Eighteen: The Little Warrior Tree	173

Introduction

The Shaman & His Daughter is a collection of eighteen inspiring short stories that explore the deep bond between a father and daughter as she grows from five to ten years old. Angel-Girl is her father's daughter: a true seer whose gifts have been nurtured by her father since she was born – she is a shaman and spiritual warrior in training. However, you won't find them living deep in the Amazon but in Arizona with teacher-parenting meetings and weekly shopping at Safeway! I hope the stories are relatable to your life and the core challenges we all face day to day – to keep picking ourselves up and moving forward. Life can be tough. There are secrets and magic and answers within the world of shamanism. All we need is a good guide! The stories in *The Shaman & His Daughter* reveal how the pure spirit of a child can sometimes lead the way.

Even though I've used many autobiographical aspects of my thirty-year-career as a shamanic healer and spiritual teacher in these stories, *The Shaman & His Daughter* is a work of fiction – which gave me the ability to share universal truths. I have used my own name, *Gregory Drambour*, in the stories because it just felt right inside me to do that – and that is one of the book's messages – listen to your wisdom! Trust it! And ultimately, giving the father in these stories my own name allowed me to draw from my own life in a more personal way.

I would invite you to read these short stories from the beginning as you would any novel, for in that way you can travel with Angel-Girl on her journey of apprenticeship as a shamanic healer. Reading sequentially, you'll also be able to follow the father's arc of learning to be a single parent as he recovers from devastating loss. You will get to see how even a master healer and successful spiritual teacher can be tested and overwhelmed by life. I was committed to being transparent in the writing and dug deep into my own experiences to convey his struggles. I have found in my own journey that when my teachers shared their personal stories, I was able to connect more with their humanity, and it had a lasting impact on me.

But though this book charts a father and daughter's mutual journey of self-discovery and spiritual growth, each story also stands on its own. So, if you're curled up under the covers, or flying on a plane, or in a waiting room somewhere and you really need to feel your soul smile – just open to any story and I promise your heart will soar!

Gregory Drambour
Magic Kingdom (Sedona), Arizona
July 2017

Chapter One

The Fairy People
(Angel-Girl at five years old)

The world felt like it ended for me three years ago when my wife Shyheart was killed in a car accident. In that moment I truly wanted it to end so I could get to the afterlife and be with my soulmate and best friend. My life as a shamanic healer and spiritual teacher was put to the ultimate test.

The waves of pain and horror from losing her have begun to lessen over time. Perhaps it's because I have become really good at knowing what can distract me so that I'm not swimming around in sorrow. The list is short: writing, working with clients in my shamanic practice, and being with our special five-year-old daughter. Angel-Girl really doesn't remember her mother. I envy her that in some strange way, but I know she feels her mother. That's just who my daughter is, someone who feels deeply.

The sadness wave is definitely looming out there today on what would have been our twelfth wedding anniversary. I sit in my home office, watched over by the red rocks of Sedona, doing my best to distract myself by working on the weekly spiritual newsletter to my subscribers. The Danish teak desk I sit at always comforts me. There's something about its organic quality that resonates with my soul. What a challenge it was all those years ago to give myself permission to spend the money on such a thing of beauty. It was a gift to myself on my twenty-fifth sobriety anniversary. But even that victory couldn't immediately overcome some long-standing poverty consciousness. It took a few months to convince myself to buy it. But whenever my Angel-Girl sits coloring at the desk with me, the sadness doesn't have a chance.

When I'm writing, my door always remains open in case Angel-Girl needs me. But if the door is closed, she knows I am on the phone with potential clients or doing a follow-up with my retreat clients and should not be interrupted unless it's a super-emergency. It took her awhile to learn that having ketchup in her nose does not constitute such an emergency! My clients come on spiritual retreat because they want to move forward on their spiritual path and reconnect to their innate wisdom; they are stuck and want to create a breakthrough.

Since I'm writing today, the office door is open. Suddenly, I hear Angel-Girl's excited voice call out "Daddy!" from her cozy bedroom across the hall with its dozens of stuffed animals and gallery of drawings. "Angel-Girl!" I call back. These shout-outs have become an ongoing routine with us. I love these moments and I think Angel-Girl does, too. Even though I can't see her, I stop what I'm doing and turn my chair so I'm facing the door.

"Daddy, the Fairy-People are flying around my room again!"

"Cool!" I call across the hall. Because of the hardwood floors throughout the house, our voices carry easily.

"They are flying around my bed in a circle. There are seven of them! What do I do?"

"Well, first say hello to them," I advise.

"I did that already, Daddy, like you taught me!"

"Did they say hello back?"

"Yup! Together, they all said, 'We greet you, Angel-Girl!'" Then she asks me with wonder and surprise, "But, Daddy, how do they know your special name for me?"

This is the big challenge when you have a daughter who is clairvoyant or "sees" – she asks tough questions! I look through the back window for a moment, gazing at an old juniper tree, which is the gateway to a winding magical trail into the mountains.

I reply, "You could ask them how they know."

"Oh, okay." Then I hear her whispering as if it's important not to scare the Fairy-People, "How do you know my special name?"

There's a pause, and then Angel-Girl calls out to me, "They said, 'Everyone knows!' Who is everyone?"

"You could ask them that too!"

"Okay." Then I hear her put this question to the Fairy-People in a soft, respectful voice. She listens for a moment and then in response she says, "Oh!" She reports to me,

"They said, 'All the Fairy-People know! All over the world. One knows, all know.'"

"One knows, all know! I like that!" I say.

She goes quiet for a long minute and I wonder what's up. "You're quiet over there."

She calls back, distractedly, "They were giving me flying instructions."

"Awesome! Is it hard?"

"The upside-down part looks fun!" she says, psyched. I chuckle to myself. She continues, "They are all flying upside down to show me how to do it. Once in a while they bump into one of the bears or my drawings of dinosaurs and then giggle! I'm getting dizzy."

The bears are her stuffed animals. I think for a moment and wonder, *Is she getting dizzy from watching the Fairy-People fly upside down or because she is flying clairvoyantly?*

"Angel-Girl, are you flying around right now with them?"

She calls back, "I'm not flying yet. I am standing on my head in the middle of my bed to see them. But I keep falling. It's a good thing I have pillows all around me. I told you buying more pillows was a good idea!" She has a thing about having lots of pillows. I finally got that they make her feel emotionally safe and protected when I am not around.

"Oh, okay," I say. I turn my head upside down to feel what she's feeling. Yup, you do get dizzy!

"My room looks much different upside down," she tells me.

"Like how?"

"Don't know how to explain it. But do you think that's why the Fairy-People fly upside down sometimes – to see stuff differently?"

My sweet daughter's wisdom floors me and I sit very still for a moment, hardly breathing, and so deeply grateful for this sudden insight: to see stuff differently!

"Daddy, you there?"

"Always, my beautiful Angel!"

"When you go flying with your eagle-brother, do you run into the Fairy-People?"

"Do you mean like bump into them in the sky?"

"No, Daddy, don't be silly! I mean like see them."

I shake my head, thinking this is too complicated to explain but then the obvious occurs to me! The simple truth: "That's a great question! No, I have never seen them when I am flying with my brother."

"Well, keep your eye out for them when you are flying," she adds solemnly.

"I will, that's a good idea," I assure her.

"Maybe you could fly upside down together. I know how important the Fairy-People are to your job. I wouldn't want you to miss them."

"No, I definitely wouldn't want to miss them." Three weeks ago a high-level executive encountered the Fairy-People on a sacred shamanic journey with me in the wilderness. She was here to deal with serious work alcoholic issues; she had barely taken a vacation in thirty years and the idea of "playing" was tantamount to a mortal sin. When she was suddenly surrounded and embraced by the Fairy-People and their playful, child-like energy, she began to cry and exclaimed, "Oh my God, I forgot what it felt like to play!"

There's a long silence from Angel-Girl's room, and then she says, "Daddy, they are sprinkling the fairy dust like they did before. It's really pretty." Then, she adds awestruck, "It's gold! They are putting it over the cover to my bed, the one with the little bears on it. And some over Mommy's picture."

I smile deeply, knowing how special it is for the Fairy-People to honor my daughter with this blessing again.

I tell her, "It means they like you very, very much."

"I like them too – a lot!" After a long moment, I hear her whisper, "Okay, I will tell him…Daddy?"

"That's me!" Another one of our routines

With deep seriousness, she says, "They all stopped flying and told me to tell you that you are their brother, and their hearts are full. You honor them. One knows, all know."

A rush of emotion fills my eyes with tears. I'm reminded again of who I am and the deep honor I feel for the gifts I was given to be able to see and feel life forces beyond this world and to help people. I try my best to get the words out through the tears and say with bowed head in deep respect, "A Ho, my brothers and sisters of the Fairy-People, A Ho." Following the Native American tradition, we say "A Ho" when we have no words to describe the depth of our feelings.

I hear Angel-Girl's proud little voice, "They said, 'A Ho,' my Daddy."

Like I said, brothers and sisters, sometimes the sadness doesn't have a chance!

Chapter Two

Visiting
(Angel-Girl at five years old)

On a stormy Saturday afternoon, Angel-Girl appears at my study door and announces with the anticipated joy only a five year old can have, "Daddy, I'm ready to go visiting!"

I look over and see she is dressed head-to-foot in bright yellow rain gear. Her rain hat, coat, and galoshes are all yellow, and she looks like a character in a Norman Rockwell painting! Angel-Girl has long, thick, dark-brown hair, high cheek bones and blue eyes like her mother, and a petite frame. Three times a week on Mondays, Wednesdays, and Saturdays, we go on a hike and talk to the Plant, Rock, and Tree-People and the Old Ones. She calls it "visiting," a word I like very much and one she picked up from her warrior mother, Shyheart, who was from the Midwest. I've always thought this kind of "visiting" represents the community-feeling you still find in the more rural parts of the country.

When my daughter was three years old and we began these "visits," I made a deep vow that no matter what was going on I would keep to our schedule of hikes together. My favorite author, Andrew Vachss says, "A father is not a father by blood or what he says, only by what he does" – and nothing will make me break this vow – nothing. This is the Warrior Code.

I peer out the window to check the weather and see it's literally coming down in a curtain of rain! I say to her, "It's still raining pretty hard, baby, maybe we should hold off until it clears a little."

"I know, Daddy, but the Raindrop-People yelled in through my window at me. They want to know when we are coming out to play with them. They're waiting! They like it when we play with them." My daughter is very serious; she feels the heart of everything, even the rain. I can hear the real concern in her voice.

"They're waiting?" I chuckle.

"Yup, that's what they said," she confirms with conviction.

I think a moment. "So if they are waiting that means it will keep raining until we play with them?"

"That's pretty much the deal," she quips.

"What!" I exclaim in shock. "What's our rule about using my parent-ickiness against me?" This line, "That's pretty much the deal," is one I use on her when I have to be firm about something. She refers to it as the "parent-ickiness." She's so smart, she remembers everything I say.

"Oh, sorry, I forgot," she says, trying to suppress a giggle.

"Uh huh," I try not to smile but I just can't help myself.

"What they want is important too, Daddy."

"Yes, it is my Angel – yes it is," I say reassuring her.

"You taught me to listen to everybody," she reminds me graciously, no hint of attitude.

I nod, smiling, so grateful that somehow, someway, I was lucky enough to feel the importance of really listening to the world and everything in it, even the Raindrop-People. The Holy Men, my teachers and brothers, awakened this in me.

She reaches down behind the door and suddenly holds my blue raincoat in her arms, "I brought your special Blue-Marmot-Bear coat, Daddy." This is a secret code of ours: blue is my soul color, Marmot is my favorite outerwear, and bear equals "cozy," as in teddy bear. She knows that since it doesn't rain a great deal here in our Magic Kingdom of Sedona, I jump at any chance to wear this coat. I am a great believer in colors being able to heal people or simply make you feel good. I was lucky enough to spend some time with Dr. Hazel Parcells, considered one of the grandmothers of naturopathic medicine. She lived to be 106, so I figured she knew some stuff! Periodically, she would be raided by the FDA, and she always used to say to me, "Greg, they can take everything away from me, but I can still heal people with colors." There is an old joke in the alternative medicine community, "If your doctor has been paid a visit by the FDA, you are probably in the right place!"

Looking at my special rain coat, I say, "I don't get to wear that enough, do I?"

"No, Daddy, I know how important blue is to you. Like yellow with me!" She spreads her arms out to show me her yellowness. "The Yellow-Flower-People like it when I'm the same color as them! It makes them feel happy."

She just naturally understands how to honor the Mother Earth. In my shamanic teaching, a core principle is non-verbal communication that she embodies. It can be as simple as breathing in sync with a tree or using hand gestures to convey your feelings. This silent language can be very powerful and has a way of bypassing our thinking. Sometimes words can't hold all we want to say.

"Excellent idea, Angel-Girl! Okay! Let's go visit with the Raindrop-People!"

By the time I get my rain boots on, she is already out the back door, running between the yellow flowers, jumping in the puddles, and laughing. I step outside and hear her shout to the sky with the raindrops splashing gently over her little face, "I greet you Raindrop-People, I am my Daddy's daughter, Angel-Girl! I am Angel-Girl, your friend."

She is the vision of her mother Shyheart in this moment. I can remember her mother running out in the rain many times to do exactly the same thing. I would laugh and run out with her and we would dance under the raindrops, knowing all was well in the world. As I watch Angel-Girl, I feel my heart start to break again for the thousandth time since my wife's death. I quickly get it under control, so my daughter doesn't see. I miss my Shyheart so much in instances like this, I feel like I can't get a breath. But at the same time I feel deeply blessed to have a daughter that feels nature so deeply. So grateful to be able to witness these special times. I sometimes feel caught between these two worlds. One of gratitude, one of sadness. Both pulling at me. The sadness bringing me closer to my late wife in some strange way.

Shyheart was the truest and bravest warrior I have known. She survived a severely abusive childhood that might have caused many to travel a road of self-destruction. When she was killed in the car accident, we had been together nine years. A true soulmate. She knew my heart like no other woman I had ever been with. I had been lucky to be in relationships with strong, centered women but Shyheart gave me something I had never felt: a deep acknowledgment of who I am and especially what I do for a living. She just got me. I didn't know this was missing in those previous relationships. And I have brought this encouragement into my practice with clients; to become a master at acknowledging your partner and your loved ones.

In the first two years after her death, a day would not go by that I didn't say to myself, *All I care about is taking care of my daughter and helping as many people as I can until I meet my Shyheart in the afterlife.* I was done with everything else. That thought is fading now. I hope.

My daughter's sweet voice brings me out of my thoughts. "Daddy, the Raindrop-People are kissing my face!"

My heart smiles. "That's a beautiful way of looking at it, baby!"

A world of gratitude keeps rising up and I must let myself be willing to be pulled into it. Warriors allow their God-given willingness to translate into behavior, into action.

I say formally to Shyheart's daughter, "You have honored them on this day by listening to them, my little warrior."

"Thank you, Daddy."

I am so proud of her. I can feel myself moving into joy. I think to myself, *Willingness, brother, willingness.*

Chapter Three

The Big Boo-Boo
(Angel-Girl at five years old)

It's a beautiful Saturday afternoon here in Sedona and as I am walking by the door to Angel's-Girl's room, I hear her whisper, "That's when Daddy had the big boo-boo." She is talking about my journey of surviving Stage 4 throat cancer before she was born. I was in my late thirties when I was diagnosed. I didn't like the consequences of conventional treatment I was hearing from the oncologists. The radiation would severely decrease my salvia flow – permanently. To quote them, "Greg, you'll just have to walk around with a water bottle. It's not a big deal." After a little research, I discovered it can be a very big deal with a long list of extreme consequences. Sometimes it can get so agonizing, people commit suicide. So I opted to do an alternative program designed by world-renowned cancer herbalist, Donald Yance. At that time doing "alternative" first was unheard of. Cancer patients usually pulled that trigger when conventional treatment had no more answers for them. I decided "first, do no harm." I had great success for three years but couldn't quite get it and in the last year did chemo and radiation. A new radiation technology called IMRT had finally been introduced in a few hospitals in New York, which would protect my salvia glands. And it worked! It's been fifteen years now!

I lean into her room and ask, "Who are you talking to in here, my Angel?"

"Bear-That-Waves, Daddy."

I see she is sitting cross-legged on the bed in conference with one of the many stuffed bears that live in the house with us. The other dozen bears in her room seem to be listening too! Bear-That-Waves is a new addition, gifted to me by a very special friend. This special bear always seems to be waving at you. He has the most amazing smile, which shines a deep sense of happiness that teaches me about staying happy in the face of whatever life throws at me. Especially on the shamanic warrior's path! Message from Spirit: "You want to be on the warrior's path, brother? Then buckle up. Here we go!"

"You were telling Bear-That-Waves about the big boo-boo?" I ask her.

She shouts with total exasperation, "Daddy! You forgot our deal!"

"Oh, no, you're right." I say guiltily.

She stares at me with those big blue eyes, waiting for me to state the deal! And adjusts Bear-That-Waves so that he is staring at me too.

"No listening outside the door to secret conversations." I repeat again for the umpteenth time. Dad just can't seem to get some of these rules!

She gives me the big strict face! I bow my head and humbly say, "My apologies, my daughter."

She smiles, "Okay, but don't forget!"

"I won't, I promise."

I sit down in the big, light-green suede chair that is "reserved" for Daddy when he is visiting her room. With permission, of course. It faces her bed, which always seems to be crowded with books and drawings she is working on and of course different stuffed animals who are visiting. Her bed is bigger than most other kids have. That was her request. "Daddy, the bears and me need more room!" I never understand why parents fight kids on these simple little desires.

"Bear-That-Waves was asking me why after work you sometimes have a sad face. And I told him that was probably because you were working with a client that has the big boo-boo like you did. And you get a little sad because you want to help them so much but sometimes they are not ocean-listening."

She is blowing me away on so many levels. For a moment I don't know what to say. I didn't know she "saw" this subtle sadness. And that concerns me. I work with a lot of cancer patients and survivors and sometimes they can be very resistant to change. I have a theory that the stage of cancer is proportional to their resistance to live in their Spirit. Most prefer to dwell in their own personal thoughts. When the stakes are life and death, I can sometimes get into a "wanting" or "efforting" with cancer clients. I'm not sure what Angel-Girl means by the phrase she just used so I ask, "What's ocean-listening?"

She motions with her little hand and says, "Underneath."

"You mean deep-listening?"

She nods emphatically.

Deep-listening is listening from a quiet mind and being careful not to go into "I know-listening" or "agreement-listening" and another dozen ways we listen to our thinking instead of what the person is saying. Especially important when working with a spiritual teacher. You want to forget what *you think you know* and be a great student.

"I love that! Ocean-listening!"

"Dolphins and mermaids are very good listeners, Daddy," she states seriously.

"Yes, they are! We learned that from the mermaid documentary."

"Everyone knows that mermaids are real now!"

"I know! They have really big eyes, " I add.

"Bear-That-Waves wants to watch the mermaids."

"Absolutely! We can watch it again tonight."

"He says that mermaids speak with their hearts."

I nod, feeling that, too. "I think you're right, Bear-That-Waves! You can see it in their eyes." (It's not only little Angel-Girls that can hear the voice of bears!) "So you see I'm sad sometimes after working with clients?"

"Yes, Daddy, we don't want you to be sad." I'm thinking. *I don't want you to see I'm sad either.* And then on the other side, I have to be careful that I don't get sad if I can't help folks...Lots of stuff here!

Angel-Girl leans into Bear-That-Waves and listens deeply and then looks up at me. "Daddy, Bear-That-Waves wants to know if going through the big boo-boo helped you to speak from your heart better?"

My whole being goes silent hearing this "truth." I stare, stunned at the little bear that has helped me so much. There is no doubt that the cancer journey softened me. And I am glad it did. Despite all the good and deep work I had done before getting cancer there was still some anger inside me. Also, the need for a deeper belief in myself. Dealing with cancer for four years, mostly alone, gifted me this.

I sit down on the bed, picking up Bear-That-Waves and putting his head against mine. In a quiet voice filled with gratitude, I say, "A Ho. A Ho, my brother."

Angel-Girl crawls over to me and pats my face with Bear-That-Waves's soft, golden paw. I pull them both close, thinking about the mysteries of our world, the big boo-boo and mermaids. The warrior's path rises in front of me and I continue to walk it – but not alone, brothers and sisters – not alone.

Chapter Four

Three Leaves
(Angel-Girl at five years old)

Ten days before Angel-Girl started kindergarten I found myself pacing around the house in a lot of obsessive worry and fear. This would be my daughter's first real exposure to a large group of kids where she might be teased because of her uniqueness. I was picked on and called terrible names in school because I was different and it hurt me deeply, pulling me inside myself for a long time. The thought of anyone messing with my Angel-Girl's kind spirit and preciousness sparked a deep anger in me I have not felt in a long time. I felt horrible being so far from my usual calm state of mind and I'm sure she could sense something was off with me. I was also concerned that the teacher might inadvertently disapprove or detour her special gift of clairvoyance, which is so incredibly powerful.

    She arrived in the kitchen, which I was cleaning again for no reason, and stood studying me for ten seconds, then blurted out, "Daddy, you're very cranky." She turned on her heel and marched back to her room – I've been told!

"You're right, honey, sorry, I'll come out of it," I yelled down the hall, trying to reassure her. She wanted her cool and cozy dad back.

During the exhaustive research of every possible school, feeling pressure to make the right choice, the awareness of her mother Shyheart's absence started to grow in me again. I had thought I was moving forward, coming to deeper peace with her death. But with each click on the computer to get information or phone calls to different schools, the longing for my soulmate started to overwhelm me – we were a great team – we loved being partners in life – we shopped for groceries together, cleaned the house together, you couldn't pull us apart. I just wanted to experience that feeling of unity when I would turn to her and say, 'Baby, take a break, I got this." I started to fall into a hole. At night, I wasn't able to fall asleep; I'd just stare at her side of the bed, feeling an incredible sense of wanting that I couldn't find the strength to overcome. I was disappointed in myself because I thought I had finally let go of all these painful emotional places.

After I enrolled Angel-Girl in school, I knew I had to speak to the principal – but with each day that passed, I found myself avoiding making the call. I just didn't want to hear the words come out of my mouth in this important moment in my daughter's life; I didn't want to speak about her mother's absence from our lives. I felt the pain for my daughter so intensely – it paralyzed me. Finally, I got the principal on the phone when Angel-Girl was with the babysitter – I didn't want to take any chance of her overhearing the talk.

"Hi, Mrs. Clarison, This is Gregory Drambour…Yes, that's right, Angel's father…Well, she's super-excited to start school, but she's a little nervous too. Even though she loves to learn, she's…Listen, I thought it was important…" The loss of my Shyheart suddenly rushed up inside me and I tried to keep my voice from breaking. "Hold on, please…" I put my hand over the phone and tried to get my breath. "Sorry…yes, I'm fine…sorry…" I used all my strength to pull it together and took another big breath. "Yes, I'm here…sorry…" I whispered fervently to myself, *Come on, brother you can do this.* "Sorry…I just thought I would be important to tell you Angel's mom was killed in a car accident three years ago…thank you…well, she does pretty well, because she was only two she doesn't really remember her mom – physically I mean, but of course she is an important part of her life…Yes it is…I just thought I should call you…I'd appreciate it a lot if you would tell her teacher…thank you…"

I hung up and stood staring at nothing, feeling frozen in emotional pain. I knew Angel would be returning in an hour from the babysitter and I needed to pull it together. Suddenly, a powerful 2000 year old letting-go prayer I teach clients came into my head. So I sat down in one of the special blue armchairs that Shyheart and I picked out, closed my eyes, took a good minute to settle myself and placed my hands on my chest and said with deep sincerity and willingness, "God, I give over to you all this pain, this sadness, this wanting; I ask with you all of my heart to please take it; I am ready for you to receive it; I give it to you…I'm ready; thank you."

Right away I could feel the energy of these feelings lifting from me. It always amazes me how quick and effective this simple prayer is – it's the use of the word "give" that endows it with power – the inference is when we incorporate the phrase, "I give," we are entering into a partnership with the Creator whoever that might be to you. And it's my belief that God digs this! Also, "give" indicates we know we are responsible for these feelings – another thing, I think God likes.

Even though I felt like I could breathe again and was nowhere near as emotionally heavy, when Angel-Girl got home, she could see something wasn't totally right with me, "Daddy, are you okay?" she said, her voice filled with concern. I'm the rock she leans against.

"Yes, my Angel, Daddy is good, just a tough session with a client." She came to where I was sitting and gave me a hug. I have kept her insulated from anything I go through around her mother. But I suspect she knows what's going on with me.

"I love you, Daddy," she said in that sweet voice that was like music to me.

"And I love you a lot," I replied, appreciating the hug.

Two days before school began, I got my bearings back and decided to set up a last-minute meeting with the teacher to share my concerns. Honestly, I wasn't sure if this was motivated from my wisdom or if it was just over-protectiveness on my part. At the time I managed to thoroughly convince myself that I was definitely *not* in some sort of helicopter-dad mode. Airing your concerns is good, right?

I drove over for the meeting and felt like something was missing. But then it quickly dawned on me that I leaned on Shyheart in these moments – she was better at this kind of meeting than I was – whereas I tended to hold people to a higher standard of communication, she was good at not taking stuff personally. On other hand, when Shyheart encountered injustices or unfairness – watch out – my best advice to whoever might be trying to pull one over on her was run for your life! In those kinds of moments, I usually became reasonable and stayed level-headed. We were a balanced team.

I walked into the kindergarten classroom and stopped in my tracks – I thought, *what a cool place!* The whole room had a fun vibe. Like an explosion of colors! I knew Angel-Girl was going to absolutely love it. Her teacher was getting the room ready for the school year. She was in her late twenties, and had blonde hair and glasses. She looked fun, too, wearing jeans and a bright lavender shirt. "Hi!" she said brightly. "I'm Miss Judy." The tension I had about this meeting immediately began to ease.

"Hi, I'm Gregory Drambour, Angel's father, a new student in your class this year."

"It's nice to meet you. Please have a seat." Very gracious.

"Thank you." I found myself gazing around the classroom, just enjoying the atmosphere of "play and learning" all rolled up together. "Awesome room!" I said.

"Thank you. I love getting the room ready for the kids." Her eyes sparkled, and I felt the sincerity of her passion right away.

"Makes me want to be in kindergarten!" We laughed. "I envy you; it must be a wonderful job, teaching children at this age."

"I love it so much, I can't tell you," she said. The feeling flowing from this young woman was beautiful.

"Well, I just wanted to tell you a little bit about Angel."

"Oh yes, please." She seemed deeply curious.

"She's really a unique little girl…" I stopped. I had practiced this speech a dozen times in my head, trying to find the best way to explain Angel-Girl and our special way of looking at the world but suddenly it felt somewhat defensive and unnecessary. Then I called to Shyheart in my head, *What should I do here, baby?* I heard one single word as clear as day: *Trust.*

Miss Judy sat patiently waiting for me to continue. I decided I am just going to be honest: "You know what, I just wanted to come in and meet you, since I'm a little nervous about her going to school. This is first she time she will be with a lot of kids and away from home all day."

"That's totally understandable," she said. "I don't know a parent that doesn't feel that way."

"Well, that's good to hear," I responded, feeling better. "I understand the principal told you we lost her mom a few years ago."

"Yes, I am so sorry for your loss," she added, the compassion very obvious in her voice.

"Thank you."

We chatted a little longer and she promised she would keep an eye on Angel. There was something genuine about Miss Judy's reassurance. I could totally understand why any parent would trust her.

Angel-Girl has been at school a month now and even though things appear to being going well, my instinct tells me something is bothering her. The bad spell around Shyheart for me has passed – thankfully – it just slowly faded; new thinking always has a way of creating a different reality. Today we are out in the wilderness doing what we love to do most: exploring! We are deep in the forest, walking in a hidden, dry creek-bed of flat red rocks and various sizes of greyish-blue boulders; a canopy of trees and bushes conceal this place. Even though she is only five and half, I am always amazed at how she navigates over terrain, like she has magnets in the bottom of her feet! I love the mysterious, magical energy of this place we are hiking.

"Daddy!" she calls out to me in an excited but hushed

tone, as if she's just discovered something and doesn't want to disturb it.

"Angel-Girl!" I mimic her cautious tone. She has run up ahead as she sometimes does on our hikes and is standing in front of a giant green bush, three times her height.

"This leaf is talking to me," she says surprised.

"Just one leaf?" In my twenty-eight years of doing shamanic healing I have never had just one leaf talk to me!

"Yup, just this one little leaf." She points to it as I walk up. "It says it's just like me." I can sense by her puzzled tone she wants me to explain to her what's happening; I learned this tone of voice is her code for asking questions.

"You mean there are two cozy Angels in this forest?"

"I guess so!" We laugh and I tussle her dark brown hair.

"What else does the leaf have to say?"

"It says she is different than other leaves, like I am different." I sense something off in her voice, her eyes reflecting a subtle sadness.

"What do you mean?" She looks down, hesitant to answer. I crouch down to her height and ask, "What's going on?"

"Daddy, the kids at school are mean to me!" she blurts out, on the verge of tears.

"Really?" I feel a rush of anger – the intensity of it surprises me. This is what I feared. I keep my feelings in check. "What did they say, my Angel?"

"They made fun of me when I talked to the trees during play-time!" Hurt is threaded through every word. I can't wait to get home to call the school and I am quickly forming the confrontational words in my head that I will speak to Miss Judy. Shyheart and I were deeply committed to raising a child who honored everything. And I will not let *anything* get in the way of that. I try to keep my voice cool and focus on Angel-Girl.

"Wow, that must have felt very hurtful," I say.

She nods sadly. I pull her into my arms, giving her a hug. I take a big breath, trying to breathe out this anger, which I am wise enough to know is really fear. I try to go really quiet inside, keeping my promise to myself not to try to "fix her" but to listen deeply to her and my own wisdom. I notice that next to the leaf she pointed out are two leaves on either side; they seem to be protecting the leaf that's different. The three leaves grow out of the same branch and are separate from the other leaves. Something occurs to me. "Are all the kids mean to you?"

"Oh, no. Bobby and Sam are my buddies." She calms a bit at the mention of their names.

"Who are Bobby and Sam"

"They are twin brothers!" I can tell she gets a kick out of the idea of twins.

"They don't make fun of you when you are being you?"

"What do you mean, being me?"

"Well, when you are talking to the Tree-People, you do it because it feels right inside you."

"Of course, Daddy, the Tree-People are very smart. They have lots to say."

"You're right. But remember, not everyone can hear the

Tree-People. Can Bobby and Sam hear them?"

She thinks for a moment, "Bobby can hear them but Sam can't."

"Does Sam get upset about that?"

She shakes her head and says, "No, Sam says we are the translators and he is the protector."

I point to the three leaves. "You mean like your leaf friend here and the two leaves on either side?"

She stares at them intensely, then looks up at me and says excitedly, "It's Bobby and Sam, Daddy! It's a reminder, like you taught me!" In our shamanism, we stay open to the signs or omens or reflections in nature that are always trying to help us.

"A Ho, Old Ones," I respond.

Then, without my prompting, Angel-Girl says, "Thank you little Leaf-People for reminding me I am Angel-Girl, and thank you for Bobby and Sam and thank you for my Daddy who keeps my heart big. A Ho."

"That was beautiful! Good job!" I scan up and down the dry creek-bed and get a specific feeling in my body that tells me we should keep going and not head home. This is an aspect in my shamanic training course that I refer to as developing a vocabulary of feelings so you know immediately what they mean.

"Should we keep walking?" I ask her. I want her to feel our adventures are a partnership.

"Definitely. I like this place." Definitely is her new favorite word!

I can see she is feeling better but I'm personally not back yet. I feel an old need to be in control start to rise up in me again. I am sure many parents feel that way when they send their child off to school. There is an old adage – when you're angry, you're dumb! Trying to communicate to teachers or anyone from that place never works out.

I let out another big breath and try to come to my senses: What am I seeing, hearing, feeling, tasting, touching? It brings me back into the present, where answers can always be found. I'm reminded where we are walking – a dry creek-bed. I use these specials places to clear clients of negative emotions and energy.

"Hey baby, you want to learn something new?"

Angel-Girl's eyes immediately get big. "Awesome!"

"Okay! See how we are in a dry creek-bed?"

"Yup," she confirms, keyed up now that she is in shamanic-apprentice mode.

"So water flows through here, right?"

She nods, listening deeply.

"Now, you know when you get dirty, water cleans the dirt off."

"I like dirt!" She seems very committed to getting as dirty as possible. She told me it's because the earth likes her. As a shamanic healer, what I am going to say to that!

"Yes, I sort of figured that out. Okay, let's see. Put your hand in the red dirt here. I am sure you will love that!"

"Really?" She does a double take, like this can't be her dad talking.

"For sure."

"Cool!" She gets the palm of her hand covered in dirt and shows me. "Like that?"

"Perfect!" I uncap my plastic bottle and pour water over her little hand. "Now, see how the dirt gets washed away? We could say anger or sadness or any feeling that feels icky is like that dirt and we are using water to clear it away. That's what we can do in this place – we wash the icky away. Water is our friend – very powerful."

"Wow! How do we do it?"

"It's so easy. We stand in the middle of the creek-bed and put our arms straight out and call to the Great Spirit of the Water. We call it the Blood of Mother Earth because the world is mostly made of water. Then the water suddenly comes and we feel the water flow over us, like we are standing in a stream and it takes any icky-ness that we might be feeling. It just washes it away like it cleans the dirt on our hand."

"Can we try it?" she says, awed at the possibility that such a thing is possible.

"Absolutely. You stand there right in the middle and spread your arms out with palms facing forward, eyes closed – no peeking! And we will call the water together. I'll speak, then you speak. Ready?"

"Roger!" She shuts her eyes tight. "I won't peek."

I stand right next to her in that same position.

I chant, "Great Spirit of the Water!"

She repeats my words. It's so wonderful to hear her

sincere voice in this enchanted place.

"Blood of Mother Earth," I continue, "I ask you to please come forth and clear us of any icky-ness! A Ho, A Ho." Angel-Girl finishes right after me, and I say, "Great job! Let's stand very still and see what happens."

Within ten seconds, I feel a beautiful crystal-clear water begin to flow over us; the current has a light strength, pushing my body back a little; I can sense the water's freshness on my skin, waking up my energy. Then, as it passes over and through me, I feel the anger is pulled away from my spirit by the force of the water. It is released from me, just like the dirt being washed away. Something in me instantly relaxes, as if the pure spirit energy in me that was covered up is suddenly revealed and starts to glow. I am totally willing to let the anger be removed because I know that it will help me let go of my own need to be in control.

I know that water is used in many rituals in many faiths but using the energy of water in dry creek-beds to clear blocks or the feeling of being stuck is an idea that flowed up from inside me – it's important to follow these inspirations. That is my core mission with my students – to help them discover the unique and original shamanism within themselves.

"Daddy, I feel it!"

"Awesome!"

"The water is washing me! I like it!"

"Fantastic. Let it take any sadness you might be feeling. You can imagine the sadness is the color brown and you let the water wash the brown away."

"Okay!" She loves specific instructions, she's like a giant sponge.

I feel the last of the fear leave me. I feel lighter, more in faith that all will be well.

"Daddy, it worked! All the sad stuff is gone! Wow!"

"I knew you could do it! Okay, let's breathe in golden light like I taught you and fill ourselves up with it!"

"Okay." I hear her breathing.

"I'm all gold now!" she says proudly.

"You're a gold Angel-Girl?"

"Definitely!" She giggles.

"Okay, now open your eyes and take a look at stuff." I open my eyes too and peer at her with my "seeing" gift and she is truly looking gold! She is gazing around, checking the forest out like it's the first time she has seen it.

"Daddy, things look really different." There is nothing better than when you see or hear your daughter amazed at something you have taught her.

"How, baby?"

"More glowy. It's pretty."

"I see that too. Cool, huh? It's wild how the same place can look different." I hesitate a moment, then ask, "Do you see those kids who teased you differently now?"

She takes ten seconds to consider it and then nods her head up and down and adds, beaming with conviction, "I am Angel-Girl." I know by the confidence in her voice, she won't let anyone bother her anymore – she knows who she is. "Good girl! You got it!" I say, so proud of her.

I get an urge to go into a deeper explanation about this process but my gut says hold off – I feel it's important not to overwhelm her with too much teaching. Someday, I will tell her that when she lets go of the negative, then immediately – without any effort on her part – her wisdom and innate positive feelings will flow right up and she'll get a different and more understanding perspective. Eventually, she will understand that for each one of us, this is our default.

"Okay, now what's our next step before we head back?" I ask her.

"We thank everybody!"

"That's right! Excellent! Since you thanked the Leaf-People, should I do the prayer this time?"

"Okay," she says with a big, happy look on her face. She likes it when I pray.

I begin, "Blood of Mother Earth, Great Spirit of the Water, thank you so much for clearing away the icky-ness. We ask that you take it up into the heavens where it will be healed once and for all and forever. We especially thank the Rock-People in this special place. You have honored us. Our hearts are full. A Ho."

"A Ho," Angel-Girl confirms in that serious voice that seems filled with a wisdom far beyond her years.

I can see her spirit is shining bright again. I know personally that I just have to take it one step at a time and keep staying in my wisdom and all will be well. And whenever I need to call on her, my Shyheart is there.

Chapter Five

Safeway & the Bears
(Angel-Girl at six years old)

I usually shop at the health food store but once in a while I have to make a run to Safeway. It's the weekend and Angel-Girl and I are at picking up few household items. I have one mission in the store: to keep Angel-Girl away from the stuffed animals for sale! At home, our shorthand for referring to the dozens of stuffed animals that live with us (whether they are bears, bunnies, or dinosaurs) is "the bears." And though they are a very important part of our life, we are at full bear-capacity! So, if possible, I try not to bring Angel-Girl with me to Safeway. These shopping excursions overwhelm all my defenses against my six-year-old's sophisticated and powerful strategies to get what she wants – one more bear! Her big, sad eyes sway me every time. Thus far, it's "Angel-Girl 8, Daddy 0."

I have a specific navigation strategy through the store so that we end up on the side of the check-outs where the bears are not displayed. On this day, all four checkouts on the safe-side of the store are five deep with shoppers waiting. Once, I actually corralled the store manager and asked him to open another checkout just so I would not have to use the express-checkout next to the bears.

Today, I have to make a quick decision whether to wait in line or use the express-lane and hope I can block Angel-Girl from somehow seeing the bears. It's Pre-Valentine's Day so the bears are out in force on the shelves. I decide to use the express checkout and hope for the best. I queue up behind the only customer waiting and position my 6'1" frame between her and the bears, hopefully obstructing Angel-Girl's view.

She is totally aware of all these moves. She's too smart. But she doesn't say anything, lulling me so I let my guard down. She is so sneaky! As I'm holding my breath, silently willing the person in front of us *to please hurry up*, I suddenly hear my daughter's voice.

"Daddy, that bear wants to come home with us," she says, pointing to one cute, pink bear with a big red heart on its chest on a shelf behind me. *Here we go*, I'm thinking. I act like I don't hear her and pretend to wave to someone.

She tugs on my jacket, "Daddy?"

I wave again to some imaginary person across the store. Several people look at me, trying to discern if they know me. One stranger actually smiles, waving back!

She pulls harder on my jacket, "Daddy, those people don't know you. Stop pretending!"

Now, this is where part of me wants to say with unshakable firmness, "Not one more bear!" But I just can't go there.

I try and reason with her. "Baby, didn't we talk about this? We have so many bears in the house to watch over and take care of. I think it would be a good idea to hold off for a while on any more additions to the bear family."

"But that bear is talking to me!" she implores, already jumping ahead to playing her trump card! She knows I speak the "language of bears." This is the problem when you are a parent who "sees."

I try another tack: "All bears talk to you because they see your big heart."

She narrows her mother's eyes at me. I know this is her seeing if I am up to something and trying to trick her.

"But that bear will be hurt if we don't take him home with us. I can take care of him. I promise." She is slowly getting upset.

I take a breath, trying to quiet myself. I get a sudden idea and say, "Okay, let's go talk to the bear."

We walk over and get in front of the pink Valentine's Day teddy bear and I squat down to her height. "Angel-Girl, can I ask you something?" She is immediately suspicious. Bad dad-move! She gives me a big, stubborn frown. You parents know "the face."

I say to her, "I am going to take that cute face as a yes." She holds "the face" in place; she's tough. "Baby, did that bear tell you it would be hurt if we don't take him home with us?"

"Sort of," she mumbles, little arms fully tightened over her chest.

"I'm just asking if maybe it's possible that you think it will be hurt."

"What do you mean?"

"Well, maybe we should ask *him* how he feels."

She is starting to get the sad eyes again, sensing what might be coming. And seeing those eyes my dad-heart is trying to steel itself, yelling, *Warp power to the shields, Mr. Sulu. Hurry!* I say as softly as I can, "Why don't we ask him?"

She reluctantly says, "Okay, Daddy." Some part of me relaxes when she uses the word "Daddy." I might not be the "Evil-Caca-Daddy" on this day.

She looks directly at the little pink bear and I know she is talking to him.

After a moment, Angel-Girl says, "Pink-Heart-Bear just told me it's okay if we can't take him home, he feels in his heart he will find a cozy home." Then with a sad, accepting face, she adds, "Okay, I understand."

I give her a hug and tell her I love her very much and that she is very brave. She peers up at the little bear; I know she is saying good-bye to him. I hold her hand and we go to the line and check out quickly, then walk to the exit, with her hand still in mine; I am hoping she will be okay.

As we near the sliding doors, I feel a sudden block in front of me! I stop short and then try another step forward and get stopped again. Yup, it's a *block* exactly like the ones I sense on sacred shamanic walks with clients when Spirit doesn't want me to go in a certain direction. It actually feels like a physical barrier. Feeling and understanding the difference between what appears to be a "good idea or direction to go" and "the expressions of Divinity or what Spirit wishes" is a very important teaching in my shamanic training program.

I stand there as customers flow by us. Angel-Girl asks, "What's wrong, Daddy?"

Suddenly, I feel all the thoughts in my head go quiet, I sense a stillness around me. I know this feeling, it means the *truth* is close. The next move is always "faith" that whatever wants to flow up from the nothing-ness, will – don't try to reach for it. I glance down at my beautiful daughter. My face must have turned very serious because Angel-Girl matches my stillness. The busy sounds of shoppers around us seem to hush. Out of the silence, suddenly I understand.

"Angel-Girl, you called that little bear something?"

"Yes, that's Pink-Heart-Bear."

"You felt that was his name – inside?" I say pointing gently to my chest.

"Oh yes, I felt it in my heart," she responds with confidence, reassuring me.

I nod my head, confirming what I understood. "A Ho, Angel-Girl," I say formally. "It's traditional when one gives someone or something a special name they are forever linked to you. I apologize to you, my daughter, for not remembering this. Please forgive me." I bow softly, subtly to her. This bowing is a ritual of ours when one wants to express deep humility.

She peers up at me with surprised eyes, welling up with tears.

I announce, "Let's go get Pink-Heart-Bear. He is joining the family!"

She grabs me, hugging me close, "Thank you, Daddy, thank you."

Brothers and sisters, nothing is more important than following the expressions of Divinity and letting go of seemingly good ideas and listening very deeply to little Angel-Girls in the aisles of Safeway!

Chapter Six

Sparkly-Mind & Chocolate-Chip Cookies!

(Angel-Girl at six years old)

It's Monday afternoon and I'm sitting against a towering Arizona Cypress tree who always keeps me company when I am waiting for Angel-Girl's yellow school bus. I can feel the Tree-People are waiting for her too! My first-grader feels the trees deeply. Sometimes I talk to the big tree, asking how I am doing as a dad. It's heard a lot of Dad-freaking-out stories. My tree friend keeps it simple, "Hang in there, brother!"

 This waiting for the school bus is one of my favorite things to do. It feels important. There is a principle I try my best to live by from the author and child-advocate, Andrew Vachss: "If you can't be counted on, you can't be counted in." I want Angel-Girl to know I will be always be there for her. As soon as the bus pulls up, kids start to file out. Angel-Girl is the last off and right away I can see from her sad face that something is up. She is dressed in a white T-shirt with a happy yellow flower on it and blue jeans, which makes her sadness even more pronounced. As she walks over to me, I crouch down to her height and ask softly, "What's wrong, my Angel?"

"Nothing," she responds flatly, hardly looking at me. Since there are no sidewalks where we live, she starts walking down the side of the street near the curb, oblivious to everything. Not good.

"You sure?" I check again. She gives me a silent nod and continues to plod down the block. I usually take her mini-knapsack and carry it for her but my gut tells me to let that be. The houses in our neighborhood are a variety of Santa Fe-stucco ranch homes. The big red rock mountains frame the background in every direction. It's always quiet, and I hardly ever see people walking around. There is almost a museum quality to its stillness, a loneliness; it makes me feel Angel-Girl's sadness even more. I sense myself falling into an old pattern of wanting to fix her. It's like an energy that rushes up in me but each year since her birth, I have gotten better at resisting it and not acting on it.

As we walk the two blocks back to our house, I am wondering whether I should try and hold her hand. I hate it when she pushes me away and today things feel risky. I do my best not to take such rejection personally but sometimes it feels like being stabbed in the gut. But I am sensing a specific feeling inside me that I know to mean *it's okay*. Even though my work as a healer and teacher is about helping folks develop and trust this vocabulary of inner-feelings, I still feel nervous as I reach out for her hand.

When she gladly puts her hand in mine, some part of me breathes! I remind myself not to go into an interrogation. It took me a few years to *start* to let go of my desire for her to be happy all the time and to fix it when she's not. I feel the desire lurking out there, so I take a quiet breath that she won't notice, letting it go.

After a few minutes of walking in silence, she blurts out, "Daddy, the kids were mean to the teacher!"

We stop, standing in the street. "Really? What happened?"

"Our teacher, Miss Sands, was sick today, so we had a sub teacher, Mrs. Cooper. The kids made fun of her when she wasn't looking! Like when she was writing at the blackboard. They made bad faces."

"Why did they do that?" I ask, looking down at her, making sure she knows I am really paying attention.

"She has metal things on her legs," she says with tears starting to form in her blue eyes.

"You mean like braces?" I inquire.

"I guess so and she has things that hold her up..." She mimes something around her hands and forearms with a pained face, which I think reflects what she imagines to be the kind of pain the teacher is feeling.

"You mean crutches?"

"I think so. She doesn't walk real good," she says.

"Oh, that's too bad," I say, sadly.

"Why are people so mean?" she asks me with a hurt voice, longing for an answer.

"That's a good question. I can see it hurts you a lot."

"What should I do, Daddy? She was really nice. I liked her a lot."

"Well, I guess the first question you want to ask yourself is, am I in sparkly-mind or mud-mind?'"

"What's that?"

"Well, sparkly-mind is when we are in a good mood and smiling inside and mud-mind is when we are in a bad mood and feel icky."

"Definitely mud-mind!" she exclaims.

"Okay. Then we don't do anything right away because when we are in mud-mind it's very hard to hear any good ideas inside. It's like the mud is blocking us. So we wait for sparkly-mind to come back, like it always does. And suddenly, we have all sorts of good ideas about what to do. Make any sense, my Angel?"

She nods reluctantly, seeming to feel a little better. "I don't like mud-mind!"

"Me neither." I wait a few moments and then ask her, "Should we have a snack and then go hiking?"

"Chocolate-chip cookies?" she asks expectantly.

"You got it!"

"Yay, chocolate-chip cookies!" She shouts, running ahead and going through door in the garage to the kitchen. Fifteen minutes later, we are out on the hiking trail behind the house and into the red rocks. Our house sits against the national forest. My wife Shyheart and I had been looking for a house for a solid year and couldn't find anything. We had finally given up and were checking out another rental in this neighborhood. We saw right away the house wasn't for us and as we got back in the car, Shyheart stopped and looked off towards the mountains. I had seen this faraway look many times and knew it meant she was "seeing" something.

She said, "Baby, let's drive down the block a little ways." As we drove down the street, she said with urgency, "Make a right here!" When we made the turn, I could see there was a For Sale sign up ahead, next to a red-brick home.

We drove up to the house and stopped and then she whispered, "Right here, my love, right here." We got out and immediately walked in the backyard and saw it was a gateway to the red rock mountains. We knew we were home. That was my beloved Shyheart.

On our hike, Angel-Girl has brought along one cookie, which she has tucked carefully in a plastic baggy in her coat pocket. This is a ritual of hers. She waits for the right moment to offer the Old Ones a cookie! We walk along for a while in quiet, studying the agave plants that are starting to grow, their tall, flowering stalks emerging from their center leaf. They can reach up to fourteen feet and then bloom a yellow canopy of flowers. They are special to us. I have always felt like they are protectors and I've often found them guarding many of the sacred places or sacred areas of power I have discovered in the wilderness. It's like they're tall sentinels in the high desert, watching over us.

"Daddy, look at this!" Angel-Girl says, pointing at the ground just off the trail. I walk over and look down and see a big paw print clearly outlined in the soft red soil between two small red rocks. Much bigger than the print a dog would leave.

"Wow!" I exclaim. "Good eye, my Angel!" I study the print. "You know what? I think it's a mountain lion track!"

"Really!" she says.

"Yup. I heard they come down from the mountains once in a while."

"Cool!"

"Let's follow her path a ways," I suggest.

"We can do that?" she asks, excited.

"Oh yes, it's how we learn about the mountain lion."

We walk slowly, examining the line of the tracks as they weave a path through green manzanita bushes with their network of bright copper branches and green leaves; they are starting to show their tiny red berries.

"Look at this, do you see how one paw drags?" I point it out to her with my finger. She studies the track closely, trying to see what I'm showing her.

"I see it! What does it mean?"

"Well, it could mean she's hurt."

Angel-Girl looks up at me, suddenly alarmed, "She's hurt?"

"I'm not sure, my Angel."

She eyes the track again, looking deeply. I feel her going

very still. She gets down on her knees and places her little hand gently inside the paw print and closes her eyes. I slow my breathing to match hers. She is being her father. With a start, she snaps her eyes open, looking super-surprised.

"Daddy, remember when you told me when a picture comes into my head real fast, it might be important?"

"The occurring moment."

"Yup!"

"Did something come to you?" I ask.

She nods emphatically and says, "You're right, it's a girl lion. She is okay. I saw her walking in the woods, big trees all around her. That's just the way she walks! She is very pretty with golden fur. Then she turned and looked at me, like she knew me. She has big eyes. I felt her heart."

I am so proud of her. "Excellent, baby!"

"Thanks, Daddy!"

Then she steps firmly on the soft soil next to the paw print, creating a deep impression of her hiking boot. She reaches in her pocket and takes out the chocolate-chip cookie and places it between her footprint and the big paw print. As she covers the cookie with her hand, closing her eyes, she says, "This is for you, little mountain lion. My daddy made them, they are very yummy! My footprint is right here next to yours so you won't get lonely."

"Good job, my Angel. If you honor them, they will honor you."

"I remember, Daddy," she says, smiling.

The next morning, Angel-Girl runs excitedly into my

room, still in her pjs. She's obviously forgotten our "rule" about not waking up Dad from a dead-sleep unless the house is burning down. "Daddy, Daddy!"

"What's up? You okay?" I say, trying to stretch as I shake off the haze of sleep.

"I woke up with sparkly-mind!"

"Awesome!"

"I know what to do about the new teacher, Mrs. Cooper!"

"Fantastic!"

"But it's a surprise. Can I have permission to use some of the silver-stuff in the kitchen?" she asks me, her face full of hope that I will say yes.

"Silver-stuff?"

"That you put food in."

"You mean the tin-foil?"

"Yup!" She's so amped she is bouncing up and down.

"Okay, I guess." I quickly try to process how she could hurt herself with tin-foil.

"Thank you, Daddy!" she shouts, bolting out of the room. I hear her running on the wood floors down the hall toward the kitchen and then back into her room, closing the door. She calls out through her bedroom door, "No peeking!"

"Okay!" I yell back.

Fifteen minutes later, as I'm making our morning smoothies, I hear her walk into the kitchen behind me. I turn around to find her looking at me with a giant smile.

I do a double take because I see something bright around her legs. I focus in and see that she has taken the tin-foil and rolled it like a thick bracelet around the ankle of each leg and then another bracelet below each knee. Then she connected the two bracelets on each leg with a straight column of rolled foil running down each side of both calves. It takes me a fast moment, and then I get it. She is matching the teacher's leg braces. The path without words – the language of a warrior.

I have seen beautiful, breathtaking things in my life, brothers and sisters, but never anything like this. I stand up very straight, my eyes filling, having no words.

"I am ready for school," she says, beaming at me.

I open up my arms and she runs into them. As I give her a hug, I whisper, "You have a big heart, my Angel! Thank you for choosing me to be your Dad."

Chapter Seven

St. Jude
(Angel-Girl at six years old)

I'm in the kitchen in my nightly confusion about what to cook a six year old for dinner. I can "see" into alternative worlds but when it comes to cooking – not so good! Suddenly, I hear Angel-Girl yell in alarm from the living room, "Daddy!"

I run in and find her sitting on the big couch watching television, holding Bear-That-Waves tightly against her chest.

"What's wrong, baby?" I ask.

She's crying and points at the flat television screen. "Daddy?" There's a questioning, disbelieving tone I have never heard from her before.

I look at the television screen and it's a commercial about St. Jude Hospital for Children. They are showing a picture of a six-year-old girl with no hair, obviously very sick, with a tube coming from her arm. I know what's wrong right away.

I sit down on the couch next to her. She gets in my lap, burying her face in my chest, still crying. I let my heart rate and breathing slow, trying to calm her.

"Daddy, kids get the big boo-boo?" she asks me through the tears. She refers to my stage 4 throat cancer journey as the "big boo-boo."

"Yes, they do, baby," I say, quietly.

"They look like they hurt," she cries.

I nod again, not having words in this moment, feeling the terrible sadness of any child suffering.

"It hurt when you had it?" she asks.

How do I tell my child that the night after my tenth radiation treatment I was literally screaming from the pain? It was like someone took a red-hot poker and stuck it into the back of my throat and left it there. I was alone, on my knees, crying, begging God for help. And in that moment, after four years of being challenged with cancer, I made a resolution: I was done with treatment. It was too much. To this day I don't know how I made it through the night. The next day my radiation oncologist implored me to come in and talk. We discussed my options, and I made the decision to trust him and kept going with the treatment. I wouldn't still be here if I hadn't taken that leap f faith.

"Sometimes it hurt a little, but I had great doctors, super-heroes," I tell Angel-Girl, trying to minimize what really happened.

"They fixed the hurt?" she asks.

I hesitate, remembering that special moment. "Well, the doctor and the nurses were very kind to me. And that kindness made me feel like I wasn't alone and I could get through it. And A.M.B. helped me a lot. You could say without them...." I feel myself getting emotional and stop. But she catches it. A.M.B. is code for "All My Bears," which are all the stuffed animals I had when I was a kid and continue to be with me. Angel-Girl has inherited them and watches over them. I hope to write about their power someday in a book I plan to write called *The Culture of the Bears*.

"All the bears were with you and helped you, Daddy?"

I nod, trying to pull it together, knowing if I speak I might lose it.

"Is that why you always say to A.M.B., I go – you go?"

"A Ho. They are my brothers," I say with fierce allegiance.

"Will I get the big boo-boo?"

"What? No, baby!"

"Why not?" she asks, fearfully.

Does this parenting stuff ever get easy? I wonder.

"If those kids got it, why wouldn't I get it?" Tears start to run down her solemn face again.

I am trying my best to quiet myself inside but there is a panicky feeling creeping up inside me that I might not be able to give her a reason. The last thing I want to do is to put it in my daughter's head that she is like any other child who could possibility get seriously ill. I take a breath, and have faith that something will flow up. Then an idea occurs to me. I don't know for sure if it's right or wrong but it feels right.

"Sometimes, my Angel, God has a plan we don't understand. In fact, a lot of the time! But in my heart I don't think that's the big plan for you, baby. But you know, those kids who get the big boo-boo, almost all of them are okay because of places like St. Jude." I have read that the survival rate for children with cancer is 85 percent, so I feel I'm pretty safe in saying this.

"They save them? Is that why they put it on TV so you can help them?" she asks, wiping the tears from her face, starting to grow calm.

"Yup, they are hoping folks will donate money to help."

"What's donate?"

"When you send them money to help the kids."

"Oh," she says surprised, then seems to be thinking. She jumps up and runs to her room, yelling, "I'll be right back!"

She comes back out, holding her teddy bear piggy-bank out to me, "Daddy, how many kids can we save with this?"

When I see my daughter standing there holding that piggy-bank, I am so deeply grateful that I didn't stop the cancer treatment and that I'm still alive to witness such a thing of beauty.

"A lot, my Angel! In fact, why don't we set it up online that we send them money every month automatically?"

"Really! We can do that?"

"Absolutely!"

Angel-Girl's face brightens. "And when we go hiking, can we ask the Tree-People to watch over kids with the big boo-boo? The Tree-People are very smart."

"Great idea!"

"I feel better now, Daddy! What's for dinner?"

"What's for dinner?" I repeat, buying time. I've forgotten all about dinner. "What all Angel-Girls love!"

"Brownies?"

I laugh. "Nooo! Lots of vegetables, especially spinach!"

"Icky!"

"Icky!" I reply, tickling her, hearing that Angel-Girl-giggling, which is right up there with hearing A.M.B. whisper those many years ago, "We are here, our brother, hang on, hang on. You go – we go."

Chapter Eight

The Deer-People
(Angel-Girl at seven years old)

It's Sunday and I'm in my study working on a new tutorial for the Shamanic Online Training Program. This particular series of lessons helps students develop a deeper relationship with the Old Ones in nature, reminding them that they are always present to help – all one has to do is ask and then let go and be in faith. The key to nurturing that relationship is one simple phrase: if you honor them, they will honor you.

I hear Angel-Girl call out to me from her room: "Daddy, Daddy! There is a deer looking at me!"

"There is a deer looking at you?" I shout back, surprised.

"Yes! Definitely!"

"Are you dreaming-on-purpose?" This is our phrase for shamanic journeying where one goes into a deep meditative state to visit other worlds.

"No, the deer is outside my window looking at me!"

"Cool!" I respond.

"Come and see, Daddy. He has those things on his head like in your book!"

"You mean antlers?"

"Yup!" she exclaims.

I get up to cross over to her room and hesitate because having seen quite a few deer in our backyard, which is really the forest, they can sense movement through the windows and scurry away. It always makes me happy when the Deer-People come close to the house. And once in a while, they will sleep outside my bedroom window; the Holy Men would say this is a great honor – they feel safe.

"Angel-Girl, how far is he from your window?"

"He's on the other side, looking right at me!"

"And where are you in the room?"

"Right in front of him! We are looking right at each other! He is staying very still, and his eyes are very big!"

As quietly as possible, I walk into the hallway and stand to the side of Angel-Girl's door. I know if I even try to catch a quick glimpse it might scare the deer off. I try to visualize what's happening.

"I am right outside your door, Angel, but I will stay here so I don't scare him." I slide down the wall and sit cross-legged on the wood floor to get comfortable.

"What do I do?" she asks.

"Let me think about it for a moment."

"Okay." Then I hear her say quietly, "I am Angel-Girl."

I chuckle. Of course, introducing yourself is a great first step. "Good idea, baby!" I say.

"Like you taught me, Daddy!"

I am so tempted to take one little peek because what

she is describing is so amazing but the Deer-People have extraordinary senses and may feel threatened.

"The deer is talking to me in my head!" Angel-Girl announces.

"Fantastic! What did he say?"

"He said he's seen me in the forest! " she says excitedly. "Should I talk to him in my head like he's doing or out loud?"

"Whatever feels good to you, my Angel."

"Okay! I'll talk to him out loud so you can hear."

"Awesome!" I respond.

She asks the deer, "Were you hiding when you saw me?" A moment passes and she says to me, "He said he's seen me a lot. And that he's not really hiding but being still. He likes being still."

I hear her say to the deer, "I like being still too and listening to the Tree-People. My Daddy and I do that a lot." Another moment of her listening and then she says, "Daddy, the deer said that he could feel my stillness from far away. I'm not sure I know what that means, but I like it!"

"If you like it that's all that matters. Some stuff can't be understood."

"Okay!" Then I hear her say in a sweet voice, "Thank you. That makes my heart feel happy." After a pause, she tells me, "He smiled at me in my head. I *felt* him smiling just like you taught me to *see* feelings."

"That's awesome! I am really proud of you."

"He is turning and walking away."

I feel it's safe to move into her room quietly. Angel-Girl turns around and gives me a quick look and then peers back out the window. I look through the glass and see the deer leaping over our little wall. He is a big deer, with sizable antlers. Before the deer heads towards the forest, he stops on the other of the wall and turns back, gazing at us. He seems to raise his head slightly to look over Angel-Girl's head to stare directly at me. I raise my hand, palm facing him in traditional greeting.

"Daddy, he is looking at you."

"You're right, Angel."

"He is talking to me again!" She listens for what seems like a long time and then speaks to the deer in a serious voice, "Okay, I will remember." She raises her little hand, formally saying goodbye. The deer scurries into the trees, disappearing from sight.

"Seems like he said a lot before he left, baby."

She turns around and peers at me as if she is seeing something about me for the first time. "Yes, he did, Daddy." She puts an emphasis on "Daddy" in a strange way I can't interpret. Her eyes start to glisten with tears. I hold myself back from asking her what's wrong, surrendering into the quiet inside me.

"He called you your special name, " she says, surprised the deer knew.

That tells me that whatever the Deer-People said is serious. I'm so proud that Angel-Girl can hear the Deer-

People so clearly and specifically. I'm very curious about what he said but I remain silent. It is better to let her tell me in her own time.

She closes her eyes and I sense it's so that she can focus and remember exactly what was told to her. "He said The Deer-People and the Old Ones see that I am the daughter of Bear-That-Walks-Softly-On-The-Earth. And it is good."

She opens her eyes quickly to see my response. I nod gently. My Spirit stays very still, knowing she has more to say.

She continues, her little voice full of concern, "He said that I, Angel-Girl, am a blessing from the Old Ones to my father who walked softly but in sadness." I stare at her, stunned beyond words.

She adds, "He said, 'Our hearts are full that Bear-That-Walks-Softly smiles in his heart again. It is so. A Ho.'" Then, surprised, she asks, "Were you sad, Daddy?"

"Sometimes, my Angel, just sometimes, not all the time," I answer, worrying this will upset her.

"How come?" she asks.

"Boy, that's a good question that needs a big answer." I go quiet for a moment, letting the words come to me. "You know, baby, when we lost your mom it was pretty hard for me."

"But because I'm here with you, you're not sad anymore?" she asks wanting confirmation.

Afraid that the emotion will overwhelm me, I just nod

my head yes instead of speaking. She sits in my lap, and wraps her arms around my neck, "You are the coziest bear in the world, my Daddy. You go, I go."

I squeeze her tighter, no longer able to hold back the tears and respond in our special code. "I go, you go – you go, I go."

With my vision a little blurred from the tears, which won't stop coming, I peer over Angel-Girl's head to where the deer merged with the trees. and I suddenly understand that he was one of the Old Ones. In this moment, I feel so deeply grateful that for all these years I was able to honor my true Spirit, the true Greg. Because in my true self, I just naturally know to walk softly on the blood and bones of my ancestors and to endeavor to make each step a gentle prayer. If you honor them, they will honor you. And I feel honored to be Bear-That-Walks-Softly-On-The-Earth, father to Angel-Girl. It is so. A Ho, Old Ones, A Ho...

I wish you the same, brothers and sisters: the courage to honor the True-You and if you are very lucky you will be blessed with an Angel, too!

Chapter Nine

Faith
(Angel-Girl at seven years old)

My daughter should be arriving home any moment. She had to stay late at school to rehearse a play the second graders are putting on. I had a session with a client so one of her classmate's mothers offered to drive Angel-Girl home. I'm preparing food for our father-daughter "expedition" this weekend into the red rock mountains. We refer to them as expeditions when we set out like explorers into unknown areas – even though we're only gone for three hours! And of course, all expeditions need to be supplied with "pbjs" and chocolate-chip cookies!

There is a strange thing that happens inside me that I enjoy when a car makes the turn down our dead-end street. I feel its approach. I just sense it; it's as if the air in the house changes. It freaks Angel-Girl out! "Dad, how did you know the mailman was here?" or I tell her to go open the garage – the plumber's here – and he's just driving down our road! There is something about this sensing-moment that makes me feel one with the world. And again today, I get the sense of a car driving towards the house so I walk out to the front yard and see her ride coming down the street then swing a U-turn to drop her off. Angel-Girl jumps out and I wave thanks to the mother. As my daughter walks over to me I see something isn't right; her face is all scrunched up in anger.

"Hi," I say. She stares at me with fierce eyes like I've done something wrong, then she runs past me into the house.

"Hey, what's going on? Hold up!" She ignores me. I follow her into the house and close the door and she's standing in the foyer with her little fists balled, waiting for me.

"Why is Mommy dead?" she screams at me.

"What?" I stare at her, shocked.

"Who killed her?"

"What's wrong, baby? What's this all about?"

"Why don't I have a Mommy?"

Oh, my God, I am thinking. *What is this all about suddenly?* Since the beginning, she's always seemed to have a wonderful understanding and acceptance that her mother is in heaven.

"Baby, let's calm down."

"No!" she yells, throwing her book bag on the ground. "Who killed her?" She stares daggers at me.

"No one killed her. It was no one's fault." I try to keep my voice very calm in hopes it will settle her down. It was a woman driving the other car, another mother actually. It was decided she was not at fault.

"Then, it's God's fault! I hate him!"

"What?" This is so far from her usual demeanor, I'm blown away.

"I'm a good girl. I deserve a mother. I didn't do anything wrong."

That she would even think such a thing scares me. "Come on, baby, let's calm down."

"NO!" She runs to her room and slams the door and I hear it *lock*. Something I have never heard…ever. This chills me.

I say through the door, "Angel-Girl, I can tell you are really upset big time. What's going on?"

"Leave me alone!"

I stand there stunned. My daughter does not have meltdowns like this. Staring at her door, I'm really not sure what to do.

"Go away!" she yells, her voice still at a fever pitch.

"Okay," I say reluctantly. "I am here if you need me."

Feeling dazed, I walk slowly down the hallway to our living room, noticing the two teal swivel armchairs that sit across from one another in front of the fireplace. They rest on an amazing, blue-silk Tibetan rug. The chairs always comfort me, center me. In fact, Shyheart and I used to sit in them together; it's where we had our *big* talks. I say to myself, *Just sit for a moment, brother.*

I sit down and take a big breath, trying to get my bearings. Part of me suddenly wishes for a parenting manual with an index where I could look up advice on "seven year old who locks herself in her room." I try to discern if it's appropriate to let that happen. But then I dismiss that idea quickly because every part of me says, *Don't force anything*.

I swivel the chair towards the fireplace and gaze at the clear blue-and-green fireglass that sparkles in the hearth. *Who killed her?* I think to myself. *Wow, what a question for a seven year old to ask.* Of course, when it happened I wanted to blame it on the other driver but it was ruled no one's fault – ice on the road and a skid. It took me a long time to accept that. I used to drive out to where the accident occurred and stand on the grassy shoulder of the county road, examining the skid marks, staring hard at the pavement as if it held the answer to "why?" Once, a policeman pulled up in his patrol car and asked me if I was okay. I told him briefly why I was there. I remember the compassion in his eyes and his words, "I'm sorry."

I returned a few weeks later; the place just kept pulling at me. I was standing in the same spot when the same policeman drove up again. This time, he pulled up on the shoulder, parked behind my car, and got out. He was a big, beefy guy, in his early forties; he looked like an ex-football player. He had his full gear on: bullet-proof vest, automatic weapon on one side of his belt, a taser on the other side. Ominous-looking. But he approached me very slowly, one could even say gently, and then said, "Mr. Drambour?"

I nodded, not having the emotional energy to push words out of my mouth. This was my third trip to the accident site; it always submerged me underneath such a dark and deep place that for a few hours it felt like the muscle to speak was gone.

"Forgive me for intruding. I just wanted to extend our sympathies on behalf of the Sedona Police for your loss."

'Thank you," I said forcing the words out.

I was still staring at the road and he turned to face the same direction with me. We stood silent for a long moment. I felt his support though he didn't say a word. Then, with the utmost respect and softness, he said, "If you want to place something special on this spot, like a cross or whatever you would like, I'd be more than happy to arrange that."

Even though I thought that was a very kind invitation, it floored me emotionally. I just simply nodded in thanks, terrified that I would lose it if I tried to speak. The pain was so overwhelming that it was like being physically knocked down. So I squatted down on my haunches to get my bearings. A few seconds later, he crouched beside me, the two of us gazing silently at the place where the accident had happened. All these years later, I vividly remember his presence next to me, and how comforting it felt.

Then he said, "I lost my wife to cancer a year ago. She was only forthy-three."

I turned, peering into his eyes and saw a reflection of my pain. "I'm so sorry," I said.

He nodded. I could see him fighting against the feelings. A place I knew very well.

That policeman is my good friend now.

As I sit in the blue chair in my living room, I sense myself slowly calming down, getting a little more centered. Is Angel-Girl having some kind of delayed reaction? Possibly. After all these years I've been able to settle into a deeper acceptance of my wife's death. I've made peace with it more. The sadness only comes for a few brief moments every couple of months. I've even been out on a date. It was a little weird; no chemistry but I guess it went okay.

Checking the wall clock, I see about twenty minutes have gone by so I walk as quietly as possible over to her door and listen.

She yells through the door, "Go away!" No lessening of the anger in her voice.

Shit, I think. I really hoped she would have come out of it. I feel the need to fix this pressing down on me.

It's getting close to dinner time so I figure I'll start cooking and maybe she will be hungry and I can engage her. The kitchen feels lonely.

When dinner is ready I say through her door, "Baby, why don't you come eat? We don't have to talk about anything."

"Mommies make dinner!" she yells.

My God! What is happening here?

"What happened at school?"

"I'm not hungry. Go away!"

"I will leave something by your door in case you get hungry."

No response. She's never shut me out like this.

I retreat to the kitchen and cover her plate with tin foil, putting it on the floor next to her door, which suddenly seems as impenetrable as a vault door.

I don't feel hungry but force myself to eat something because staying calm is important right now and not eating is a bad idea. Sitting at the dining room table without her for the first time is hard. I can't taste the food. My thoughts start going to a dark place but I breathe, and just let them float by.

After cleaning up the kitchen, I wander into the living room, stopping at the big windows to peer out at the red rock mountains. The house feels silent. I don't like it. For a moment I consider calling one of my colleagues to see what they might advise. This is really new territory for me. But I quickly reject that idea. We're not there yet.

I notice twilight is creeping down. This has always been my special hour. The Holy Men taught me that we all have a special time in the day when our power is greatest; a time that resonates with our soul. Mine is twilight. Most of my inspirational ideas have come during these hours. Something suddenly occurs to me…

I go find my tobacco pouch and then step outside through the French doors in the dining room. I don't go too far into the backyard because I don't want Angel-Girl to think I am trying to spy on her through her window. I gaze up at the sky, which is starting to turn a beautiful dark blue and pink, and I take a moment to absorb the twilight, allowing myself to feel its embrace. Sensing myself quiet down inside, I rest my hands on top of one another on my chest and say out loud, "Grandfather, it is I, Bear-That-Walks-Softly. A Ho, I greet you." Then, I wait a moment, breathing slowly, dropping deep inside myself, and continue, "I invite my Divinity with all my heart to please offer me guidance on how best to handle my daughter's pain. I will stand in faith that this will flow up from within. Thank you. A Ho." I lay a small handful of tobacco on the earth as a little offering.

This is the invitation I teach parents when they are super-stuck, suggesting that they can transpose the word Divinity for "inner-parenting-mentor." But the important part is to know that the power to have an insight flow up really rests in *letting go* after you make the invitation; this is the place of faith.

I sit down in one of the porch chairs and watch the changing twilight sky, thinking how many times I have stood making this invitation, and feeling grateful I was taught its power. Warriors stand in faith. I stay outside until it goes dark, then I head inside. As I cross over the threshold of the French doors, a memory of a conversation with a colleague suddenly comes to me: I recall him telling me that when his girlfriend drops into a low mood – no matter how low – he has faith that her innate mental health will at some point reset itself and she will come out of it. He doesn't do anything.

Okay, I decide, t*hat will be my plan. I am not going to let* *the severity of her mood make the principle of resetting not true. I am not going to let her mood scare me into getting into my head and trying to figure this out.*

I feel better. It feels right to go lay down and read a bit. I consider watching some TV, but I'm concerned that Angel-Girl might think that means I don't care.

Passing her room, I say through the door, "I'll be in my bedroom if you need me."

No response.

I lie down on top of the covers of my bed and open *A Moveable Feast* by Hemingway, a favorite book of mine. Pretty soon, I feel my eyes closing and so I lay down the book and drift off.

"Daddy?"

I'm immediately startled awake and find my daughter standing beside my bed in her pjs, holding Cody, a very special caramel-colored bunny that has been with me for twenty years. Cody is a protector, very fierce. I glance at the clock: 9:00 at night. Wow, I've been out for two hours. "Yeah, baby. Are you okay?"

"I am a big mud-monster!" She announces, super-unhappy with herself. She is making reference to being in mud-mind.

I sit up on the side of the bed and look at her and say softly, "You're a big mud-monster?"

She nods emphatically, the tears welling in her eyes. With that one phrase I know she is going to be okay. Actually more than okay: she understands that she has dropped into a bad, low mood, or mud-mind. Many of the adults I teach have a challenging time *realizing* when they are in a low mood, because anger or sadness or any negative feeling has become so familiar to them.

"You want a hug?" I ask her gently.

She shakes her head adamantly, no, and hugs Cody, her protector, tighter. It's like she's afraid of letting anyone in. And I know this because she is holding Cody in particular; she feels protected by him.

"Do you want to go make some hot chocolate with me? Cody too?"

She nods yes, reluctantly.

We head for the kitchen and I start to take out all the ingredients. My daughter stands in the middle of the floor, clutching Cody, like a little lost girl. I have never seen her this upset or confused, bewildered really. Usually, when I'm making hot chocolate or some other snack, I lift her up onto one of the stools that has a thick cushion so she can be at counter height. However, I'm unsure about doing that tonight, so I ask her first.

When she nods yes, I reach under her arms and lift her and Cody onto the stool. I continue preparing our hot chocolate, just being quiet. I feel her watching my movements, her whole being just reflects a deep sadness.

"Should we take our hot chocolate into the living room and make a tent?" This is a special thing we do once in a while. She usually loves it.

"Cody comes too." This is not a question!

"Of course. I will go get the special blanket. Meet you both there."

I retrieve my king-size green blanket from my bedroom. This is the blanket I had when I had cancer. It is very special to me and comforted me through some rough times. I also grab one of the four Native American Pendleton blankets from the closet to use on the wood floor. These pendletons have been with me a long time and I will periodically use them in healing with clients. They also have power.

When I get back to the living room, Angel-Girl is sitting on the wooden step holding Cody against her chest. She appears dazed.

I create a square formation of chairs, lay the Pendleton on the floor between them, and position my green blanket over the tops of the chairs, constructing a green tent. Then, I plug in a small, rose-quartz crystal lamp and place it inside the tent, which creates a soft glow.

"Okay, it's ready. No wait, I forgot!" I run to her room, grab a bunch of pillows, hurry back, and position them on the Pendleton blanket.

"Okay," I say, *"now it's ready."*

She crawls in through the green blanket flap, and sits cross-legged with Cody, her hot chocolate on a small plate.

"It's pretty cozy in here," I say.

She nods, the sadness still etched all over her little face. We sit quietly for a minute. I sip my hot chocolate but she hasn't touched hers yet.

Suddenly, she blurts out, "I thought I saw Mommy today." I see the tears starting to well.

"Really?"

She nods. Her mom has shown up a number of times over the years. And with her clairvoyant abilities Angel-Girl has been able to see her each time.

"Where?"

"When I was coming out the front door at school there was this lady standing by a car. I looked and I couldn't believe it – it was Mommy!" She's crying now and talking quickly, trying to get it all out. "It wasn't like when we have seeing visions – it was really her, just like she looks in all her pictures. She had long dark hair to her waist just like Mommy. I didn't know what to do so I waved but she didn't wave back." Angel-Girl is really crying now. "And this first-grade girl ran by me towards her and the lady laughed and gave her a big hug. It was *her* Mommy."

She crawls over to me and I bring her into my arms. She's sobbing as she says, "I was sure it was her, Daddy."

"Wow, I can understand why you would be so upset."

"It's not fair."

"No, it isn't."

"Why did she die?"

"I don't know, baby. For a long time, I thought about that too...a long time. I was really angry."

"Really?" She starts to calm down a little.

"Oh, yes, my Angel. Very angry. Your mom was everything to me...everything. I felt she was the gift the Old

Ones gave me when I survived the big boo-boo."

"You never told me that."

"Well, I guess I haven't told you a lot of things because something inside me told me to wait. But your Dad was in big mud-mind for a while. So I understand. I will tell you a secret. Once I thought I saw her too."

"Really? You did?"

"Yup. About three years ago. I was teaching a workshop and I noticed across the room this woman checking in at the desk and then she turned and looked at me and smiled. I swear it was your mother. I couldn't believe it!"

"Wow."

"It looked just like her and for a split second, just like you, I forgot she was in heaven. I started to walk towards her and when I got closer I saw it wasn't really her." I take a big breath. "It kind of knocked the wind out of me. For one tiny moment…" I start to choke up and breathe to stop it. "After that I was in a real bad mood for a couple of days. It brought it all back: my questions about why did it have to happen, the unfairness, the anger. And I think in that moment I just let go of trying to understand why she died because *trying to understand* made me feel so bad. Make sense?"

My daughter nestles her head in my chest, squeezing herself and Cody closer to me. I hold her, rocking her in the glow of the lamp in our green tent. Closing my eyes, I feel the silence in the room. Our brother, the wind, has picked up outside. Suddenly, a Native American chant that the Holy Men gifted me starts to flow up from within me. I sing it softly – for both of us. I can feel her energy start to soften. There are moments at the end of my life I will remember, brothers and sisters; I know this will be one of them. I finish the chant, grateful for this gift, with which they have honored me.

"Daddy?"

"Yes, my Angel."

"The Old Ones are here with us."

"You are right. I feel them. A Ho, Old Ones."

"A Ho," Angel-Girl says quietly, respectfully.

The energy in the room feels ancient. This is the feeling I get up in the Northern Plains, where I spent many years. It's a connecting-sensation to the past. Suddenly, a small vision, almost like a movie, appears to me. I watch it unfold, understanding something deeply. I want to share it with her quickly.

"I just saw something, baby."

"The Old Ones showed you something?"

"I think so. You know, there are many mysteries…many. I have seen amazing things and you have, too…right?"

"Yes, Daddy, I have," she agrees, waiting.

"Perhaps in that moment your mom projected her image onto that mother, so you could see her hugging you. Maybe you had a bad day in school. And that was her way of making you feel better. Almost like showing you a movie of you and her."

Angel-Girl begins to cheer up. "Really?" she smiles.

"Wow! She is very smart."

I chuckle, "Yes, she was. She had great power. A true warrior. In all my travels I have only met *one other* person who lived in their Spirit as much as your mom."

"Who?"

"Her daughter."

She hugs me tighter.

"Always remember, no matter where she is, you *always* have a mother, *always*."

"I won't forget, Daddy," she says with renewed confidence.

Faith, brothers and sisters, Faith.

Chapter Ten

Butterflies
(Angel-Girl at seven years old)

I lean into Angel-Girl's room and announce, "fifteen-minute Client Alert!" Today I have late afternoon appointment with a stage 4 breast cancer client in my home office. When I can't find a baby sitter for Angel-Girl, she stays home with me when I am in session. She loves helping me prep the house for the client.

"Okay, Daddy!"

Angel-Girl is dressed in a pale yellow T-shirt and her lucky light-yellow overalls. I ask her. "Isn't this about the third day in a row you are wearing your overalls?"

"Definitely. They give me ideas for my butterfly project. I have to get her ready in time."

I want to ask her what she means but I have to stay focused for the client so I say, "Makes sense to me!"

Angel-girl jumps up and goes into my office and studies its readiness. She does this with total seriousness. It just cracks me up.

"The mountain rug has got icky on it," she says. This is her code for the Tibetan rug!

"Okay, you know what to do." I head for the kitchen to make her a snack for later, when I'm in the session.

She goes into the closet and gets the sweeper and I hear her rolling it back and forth in earnest over the rug, getting all the dust.

"Anything else?" I yell from the kitchen.

"The yellow things."

"You mean notepads."

"Yup."

"Okay, go get one from the closet and a pen."

"Roger that." Once in a while, not too often, I get a very clear clairvoyant hit to let Angel-Girl meet the clients. Some of them have been veterans I have been honored to work with over the years, to help them deal with challenges of integrating back into the world. That's where she learned the phrase "roger that."

I finish making her snack and go to check her work. When I come into the office, she is adjusting the pillows on the couch, very focused on making things look perfect.

"It's cozy now!"

"Looks great! Good job!"

I squat down at her height and open my arms for another of our rituals: "Pre-client hug." She runs into my arms. "You are the best helper!"

"Thanks, Daddy." These pre-client hugs always help me get into my heart.

The doorbell rings and I stand up. "That's the client! I left your snack in your room."

"Yummy!" she says, going into her room.

I lean in and say, "Okay, I will check in on you at the halfway point." She occupies her time with drawing, school projects, reading, and the million things she is fascinated with.

My client, Cathy, has been told by the oncologists there is very little they can offer her, so for the past year she has dedicated herself to a world-class alternative protocol. She has had great success and shown almost no sign of cancer! A few months back, her numbers took a tiny reversal which prompted her to schedule a retreat with me. She knows she hasn't spent enough time on the emotional part yet. My area of expertise is identifying the possible emotional contributor to getting the cancer and helping clients clear it. As a stage 4 throat cancer survivor myself, I think cancer patients and survivors sense I understand their feelings and that helps them feel comfortable with me. And in my four-year cancer journey, I utilized both alternative and conventional treatment, so it gives me experience of both worlds.

Cathy is forty-four with three kids all under fourteen, a great marriage, and if you saw her you would never know she had a serious life-threatening cancer. She has striking green eyes and looks super-healthy and fit. Alternative protocols for cancer can be very challenging to say the least. The dietary restrictions in her particular protocol are severe and only a small percentage of folks would be able to deal with it long term. She is a hard-core warrior and has my deep admiration. Cathy is what Dr. Bernie Siegel would call an "exceptional cancer patient," willing to do what it takes!

I've been in the session with Cathy for about forty minutes when I begin sensing a core of resistance with my claivoyance that is very hidden and subtle.

"Cathy, here is the big question we chatted about on the phone: what is the behavior the cancer is trying to tell you to change and have you changed it? Since we talked has this prompted any insights?"

"Nothing has come to me. I have done so much work on this." The frustration is obvious in her voice and also the fear. I know she is really scared of the numbers continuing to increase.

"You're used to figuring stuff out?"

She laughs. "You nailed me!" It's good to see this brave woman laugh.

"Is that the behavior?"

"I'm not following you."

"Is the cancer trying to point out that behavior, the need to figure everything out? Which is really just another way of saying need to be in control."

"I don't know, I can't figure that out!"

We crack up. But I have seen this before, she is using humor to deflect. Very sneaky!

"You have come here to figure out what it is you're missing. Right?"

"Correct."

"Sometimes the way we go about healing *is* the healing. Make sense?"

She squints her eyes at me, trying to understand.

I chuckle, "You are doing it right now!"

"Oh my God, I am, aren't I?"

"Yup!"

"I am really messed up!"

"Far from it. You just saw something – that's what's important."

I see by the clock we are halfway through our session.

"Hold on a second, I have to check on my daughter."

"She's here?" I notice something in Cathy's voice. Hopefulness. This makes me curious but my sense is to leave it be for now.

"Yes." I get up and cross the hall and rap lightly on Angel's door.

"Are you okay?" I ask her through the door.

She responds with "Roger!"

"Okay, see you in a little while, about another forty-five minutes."

As I return to the office, Cathy asks, "She's okay?" Again I notice a more than interested tone in her voice. Maybe she's read my stories online about Angel-Girl.

"She's great. Something just occurred to me. Tell me if this makes sense: The awareness you are still neglecting yourself, still putting other's needs before your own makes you feel like you are doing something about these blocks. And there is no doubt you are trying to change these blocks but here's my thought: you are translating 'awareness' as *doing or changing behavior* and it really isn't. Especially in the core of the codependency."

She tries to absorb what I just said. I can see it has her a little stumped.

"Can you say that again?" This is what I look for in clients – questions!

"Absolutely. You feel you are changing, right?"

She nods in agreement.

"What I am suggesting is you are mixing in 'awareness of the need to change' with behavior you have *really* changed so it creates the illusion that you're doing more than you really are and it creates a deflection from the core work, which can be really scary. One could call them deflection-changes. Awareness is not doing. Behavior is the truth, Cathy."

She ponders that for a moment and nods to herself. "What do you mean, 'core of the codependency'?"

"Well, who or what in your life are you still sacrificing your needs for, who are you still trying to fix or needing to control?"

Though the answer is right in front of Cathy, it's very hard for her to admit it.

"Could it be your children?" I ask her, softly.

Right away she defends this, "I am much better with

taking time for myself. And I'm getting better at not trying to control the kids and letting them be."

"I am sure you are. But let's say you were at a hundred percent neglect of self before, what are you at now? Even though you may be changing things externally, how much time are you still up in your head worrying about the kids?"

"I guess still a lot. But I'm a mother, Greg, that's what we do. I can't abandon them." She starts to choke up.

"I understand, Cathy – truly. But isn't the mission to create an environment where healing is possible. And if you are in worry and fear around your children, and feeling the need to control, is that helping their environment?"

"No, I guess it isn't. What do I do?"

"Well, the first step is to understand or become aware of when you are in those places and to also stop justifying that it's okay because you're their mother. And please hear this – you are doing it innocently. Please don't judge yourself!"

She smiles, "You got my number."

I chuckle. "You have shown incredible determination and discipline with your alternative protocol but you have to show the same degree of intensity with this and you *can* do it. If I've ever seen a warrior, Cathy – you are one."

"Thanks." She sounds a little hopeful.

"When you are putting other's needs before your own more than a balanced amount of time, you are creating a block to your chi force, your life force, and that's the last thing you want to do right now."

"Okay." She seems to be getting something.

As the session winds down, I recollect the subtle shift in Cathy's voice when I mentioned Angel-Girl.

"Would you like to meet my daughter?"

"Oh yes, I would love that. I was hoping I would get a chance to meet her."

"Great! Let me go get her. Hang out a second."

I get up and cross the hall and knock lightly on Angel-Girl's room, adhering to our Father-Daughter-Rules of not coming in unless I get the "go" signal.

"Come in, Daddy!" I can hear the excitement in her voice, which I interpret to mean she knows she is going to get to meet the client. She is so sensitive she knows when clients have left or not. I open the door and see she is working on her special butterfly project.

"You want to come meet my client, Cathy?"

"Yayyy!" She jumps up and grabs my outstretched hand.

We cross the hall and walk into my office. I always notice there is a subtle vibration in Angel-Girl's hand when we do this.

Cathy is still sitting on the comfortable, green-suede couch I have for clients.

"Cathy, this is my daughter, Angel."

"Hi!" My daughter beams.

"Nice to meet you, Angel!" Cathy says, reaching out her hand, which Angel-Girl immediately takes without a drop of shyness. It always strikes me how my daughter does this with confidence, holding a person's hand firmly, not letting go too quickly and looking directly at the person. She seems to be "reading" Cathy in a way that is beyond her years.

"How are you?" Cathy asks.

"I was working on my collage for school. It flies!" I purposely stand back a few feet, letting my daughter be in her own space, not hovering or trying to parent-monitor her interaction.

"Your collage flies? Wow!" Cathy responds.

"I'm hoping." She giggles.

"What grade are you in?"

"I'm in second grade. It's lots of fun. But sometimes the other kids don't understand stuff."

"Like collages that fly?" Cathy says, smiling.

"Exactly!" We all laugh. "Have you been outside with Daddy yet?"

"No, we are going tomorrow. I am really excited."

"Make sure you say hello to the Tree-People."

Cathy leans in toward her to show she is listening close to her guidance. "I won't forget. Trees are very special to me too. I hug them a lot." She closes her eyes and hugs herself tightly to show Angel how she does it.

"Really?"

"Yes, where I live there are big giant trees. Redwoods."

"Wow! Daddy promised me someday we would go visit them. Did you know that some people climb up in them?"

"I have heard that. That would be amazing, but I might be scared to go up so high!" With each moment she speaks to my daughter, Cathy's face and eyes grow softer. She had related to me earlier that most of the time she has a wall up, and it's only with children that she lets it down. Later, I want to explore this deeper with her – why does she feel she can let her guard down with kids?

I notice Angel-Girl's eyes go into a deeper focus on Cathy. Then, with a sweet, loving, and compassionate voice, she says to her, "Do you have the big boo-boo like Daddy had?"

Cathy is caught off-guard with the question. Her eyes suddenly well with tears and she just nods, as if she is afraid to speak. Angel-Girl steps forward and wraps her little arms around Cathy, hugging her, not letting go. Cathy seems surprised, but she returns the hug. I can see tears starting to run down her face. I go quiet and close my eyes for a moment, feeling something powerful in the room. I had not told my daughter about Cathy's illness.

My daughter steps back and sees Cathy is crying. "Don't worry, my Daddy is very smart." She pulls a tissue from the box on the table and hands it to her.

"Thank you." I sense Angel-Girl feels her discomfort and says, "Do you want to come see my collage?"

Cathy glances up at me subtly to see if it's okay. I smile and nod yes.

"I would love to see it!" Cathy says.

Angel-Girl takes Cathy's hand and leads her across the

hall to her room. "This way!" she says, super-excited. She guides us to her long cherry-wood workstation where her special collage sits with various building tools and crayons surrounding it. When she was younger I saw her incredible passion for creating things, so one day I sneaked in a master carpenter, after she went to school, to build a unique work-station for her. When I was picking her up at the end of the day, I got a text from him: "Done!" He had a young daughter, too. When she went into her room to drop off her school things, Angel-Girl froze, staring speechless at the stunning 10-foot long floating desk. I said, "You hate it, I guess?" She hugged my leg in a death grip, with big tears floating in her blue eyes.

"See!" she says to Cathy.

"Oh, it's a butterfly!" Cathy exclaims, her mood already starting to lift.

"You figured it out!" The butterfly collage is about eighteen inches, wingtip to wingtip, and twelve inches long. The paper collage is stretched across some thin wire to give it the shape of a butterfly.

"Oh yes, it's beautiful," Cathy says softly, seeming to be touched by its presence.

"Thank you," says Angel-Girl. "It's not ready for a test flight yet but soon. I am waiting until the Butterfly-People are here and maybe they can help Esmeralda fly. They are coming soon." That's what she meant by getting her ready! I didn't know that was her plan and I stand there blown away. She is waiting for the Butterfly-People.

Wow!

"See, each wing has pictures of butterflies on it," Angel-Girl says proudly, pointing to the colorful array of them. "Daddy and I printed off lots of butterflies from the computer, then I cut them out and glued them close together so they are cozy with each other."

"I love that! I see you have lots of yellow ones." Cathy says.

"That's my special color. It makes my heart..." She mimes get bigger. "Do you have a special color?"

"I don't know. Maybe lavender."

"I like lavender! See!" She picks up a lavender crayon to show her. "Daddy says that colors are very important, they are like friends."

"I never thought about it like that." Cathy says, seeming to make a mental note of that idea.

Angel-Girl continues, "And then, I put lots of photos of me and Daddy in the middle where her body is and I included a picture of Mr. Roberto, who watches over our Plant- and Tree-People. He loves butterflies. So when Esmeralda flies, it's like she is taking us flying with her."

My breath catches. I get a sudden insight that applies to Cathy that I will share with her when we are alone.

"What a wonderful idea!" Cathy peers closer at the different pictures in the collage. "Who is that?" she asks, pointing to a larger photograph in the direct center of the collage. My heart skips a beat.

"That's my mommy. She's in heaven," Angel-Girl says

brightly with no hint of loss or sadness.

Cathy glances over at me, acknowledging our loss silently.

"She is very beautiful."

Angel-Girl smiles in response.

I get the vibe it's time to let Cathy go. "Okay, baby, let's say goodbye to Cathy. We have to make dinner."

"Okay."

"Thank you so much for showing me Esmeralda," Cathy says. "She is very special. And I am really glad I got to meet you."

"When we go flying, I'll ask the Butterfly-People to help the boo-boo."

Cathy hugs her and whispers, "Thank you."

I walk Cathy to the front door and step outside to escort her to her car.

"Thank you so much for letting me meet your daughter. She is very special."

"Thank you." I bow slightly. "I heard something deeply just now, can I share it with you?"

"Yes, please."

"Remember, when Angel said, 'When she flies, it's like she is taking us flying with her'?"

"Yes, that was beautiful."

"Well, what occurred to me is that right now you are trying to fly! To fly from your fears!" I see a spark suddenly fire up in Cathy's eyes – she is hearing something. I take a long moment to let her absorb that. "And when you do fly – and I know you will – you will carry your children with you! When you change, they will."

Cathy exhales a long breath, seeming to let go of something. She looks directly in my eyes and says, "There is really nothing to worry about is there?"

"No," I say softly. "In shamanism butterflies are about transformation, right?"

She nods.

I continue, "And butterflies just change naturally. We could even say they *flow* from one stage to another. They just *flow*."

Cathy's energy becomes even more still, and in a hushed, almost reverent voice, she repeats, "Yes, butterflies just flow."

"You got it." I step forward and give her a hug. "I will see you tomorrow, my friend. Awesome work today. Thank you for trusting me. Remember, every time you make that change in behavior, you tell your Spirit you are listening, you tell it you got the message the cancer is trying to give you. So, with each change you are healing yourself!"

Chapter Eleven

Looking for Led Zeppelin
(Angel-Girl at seven years old)

It's finally ten o'clock and I'm feeling like a kid at his first rock concert! I have been counting the days to this night. I'm watching the much-anticipated Led Zeppelin Reunion Concert at the O2 Arena in London on television. Led Zeppelin was a big part of my late teens. I was sent to boarding school from sixth to twelfth grade. I hated every minute of being away from home, but Zeppelin's music was always a refuge. I can vividly remember in my junior year sitting in a big upholstered chair in my friend Bob's room, listening on Koss headphones to Zeppelin's new album *Physical Graffiti* – it was like being pulled into an exotic, magical world – it filled my soul like no other music had. Something broke free inside me in that moment that I had squashed down since my first year in boarding school at ten years old – I felt the real Greg coming through. I was seventeen then and that's the year I started to learn Kung Fu and practice meditation. I was slowly rediscovering my own power. It was the beginning of my journey into spirituality with Zeppelin as my theme music!

Suddenly, Angel-Girl, looking very sleepy in her yellow pj's and holding Bear-That-Waves, walks into the living room. "Daddy, the TV woke us up!"

"I am sorry, baby, I will turn it down. I guess I got excited. It's Led Zeppelin!"

"Who's that?" she asks, rubbing the sleep out of her eyes.

"What! Who's Led Zeppelin? What are they teaching you in that school! Come over here and you can watch them with me."

"But it's way past my bed time," she responds, surprised.

"That's okay, my Angel, for Led Zeppelin we can make an exception. Bring your blanket."

"Can Bear-That-Waves watch too?"

"Absolutely!" She bounces over. I remember when I was a kid and the adults bent the rules and I got to stay up late at night where mysterious grown-up stuff went on. I would watch *The Million Dollar Late Movie* and hide behind a pillow when the scary white whale appeared in *Moby Dick*! As Angel-Girl snuggles up against me, I turn the volume back up. Led Zeppelin is playing the great song, "Kashmir." It brings me in a rush back to the parties we would have in my friend Bob's furnished basement at his parents' home on the weekends. That was the moment I started to feel like I belonged – I had friends. Twenty years later, I visited Bob, who had taken over his parents' house; he walked me down to the same basement, and we both stood there not saying anything for a full minute –

the memories of freedom filling the air.

I feel Angel-Girl studying me. "Daddy, you look different," she says as if she is a bit puzzled.

"What do you mean?"

"Happier."

That takes me aback. "Really? Don't I look happy most of the time?"

"This is different," she says, looking deeper at me. I sense her going into her "seeing" place. "Like that brown book you have with the pictures of you in it," she adds.

"You mean my portfolio when I was acting and modeling in my twenties in New York?"

"Yup. You look sort of like that but *different*." She emphasizes "different" with the same tone she uses for eating spinach!

"Different in what way, my Angel?" She really has my attention now. I can feel something hovering out there – an insight.

"Well, in those pictures you look icky," she states with a little too much confidence!

"What? Icky!" I exclaim. The truth here is I know exactly what she is talking about. Those same pictures are on my Facebook page and in the caption description I wrote, "Two years sober but still pissed!" Even though I got clean, there was still a lot of anger inside me and it centered around being abandoned in boarding schools. Despite my adamant pleas to my mother that I didn't want to go, I was forced to keep going back, always with the same promise, "If you still feel the same way at the end of the semester, you don't have to stay there." That promise went on for seven years. It took me a long time, but I finally found forgiveness for my mother and saw clearly she was trying to do the best she could.

Angel-Girl says with more unbending conviction, "You don't look happy in them, Daddy."

I smile at her persistence. "You are right, baby, I was still not very happy at that time. So how do I look different now?"

"Well, right now you look *young* like in those pictures listening to Jimmy but you also look like you're *home*." The word "home" for some reason causes me to go deeply quiet inside. I look at her beautiful blue eyes watching me in her own silence. I nod to her, affirming what she sees – I do feel at *home* listening to Zeppelin.

Then something occurs to me. "Wait a minute, how did you know the guitarist's name was Jimmy?" I ask her. "Jimmy" as in Jimmy Page, the infamous guitarist for the group.

She giggles and hides her face in her hands, then peeks at me and blurts out, "I looked it up!"

I am confused now. "What do you mean?"

"On the calendar in the kitchen for today you wrote in big letters *Led Zeppelin*. I figured it was important to my Daddy so I looked it up!"

I have been floored in my life by people's kindness and thoughtfulness but this…I hold her very tight against me,

"Thank you, my Angel. I love you a lot."

"Bear-That-Waves helped too. He is good on net-thingy," she adds.

I hug him closer too. "Thank you, buddy, you are a very smart bear."

I hear Led Zeppelin start another song and I immediately recognize familiar chords. "They're going to do 'Stairway to Heaven'!"

"That sounds cozy!" My daughter vibes with everything cozy.

"When I was seventeen years old it was like our anthem," I tell her reverently.

"What's ant–tem?" she asks me, having a hard time pronouncing it.

"Hmmm. How do I explain that? It was like the most important song to us. It just felt…so special," I say, hearing the wonder in my voice. I am taken back to one particular night at a school dance and slow-dancing to "Stairway to Heaven" with the girl everyone wanted to be with – we thought of her as the perfect girlfriend – down to earth, beautiful. In forty years I have not forgotten that dance – that intimate moment defined "Stairway" for me.

Angel-Girl peers at me, seeming to hear something important in my words, then she snuggles closer to me, holding Bear-That-Waves tightly and turns her attention back to the concert.

As if it's the most obvious thing in the world, she says, "Daddy, they are like you."

"What do you mean?" I ask, baffled by what she could mean.

"Led Zeppelin are helping you find home, like you do with clients!"

That's so enormous, I have no idea how to respond.

She adds with conviction, "After you work with your clients, they always look like they are home."

"Wow, thanks, honey – that means a lot to me." As I try to absorb fully what she's just said, I whisper to myself: *I am being Led Zeppelin.* That's just so wild! I feel incredibly grateful to do my work, and even to guide just one person home is everything.

Angel-Girl's voice brings me out of my reverie, "Bear-That-Waves likes Led Zeppelin a lot, too!"

"It's a family thing!" I laugh.

She gazes up at me, cuddled in her blanket, and says, "But don't forget about being home, Daddy."

"Roger that, my Angel," I confirm, knowing the truth when I hear it. Note to self: more Led Zeppelin! Stick with what works, brothers and sisters…stick with what works.

Twenty years later I went looking for that girl I slow danced with to "Stairway to Heaven" and I found her and married her – her name was Shyheart.

Chapter Twelve

The Meeting
(Angel-Girl at eight years old)

It's close to twilight and Angel-Girl and I are out hiking deep in the woods, following the secret paths of the forest animals. Here in the Magic Kingdom animal trails are easily navigated because there is a lot of space between trees and bushes. The forest isn't packed tight like in other parts of the country. We love exploring these trails – it feels mysterious. The towering red rocks are looming pretty close on our right. Angel-Girl is about twenty feet ahead of me and goes around a corner so I can't see her for moment. Then, suddenly, I hear her yell in a surprised voice, "Daddy!"

I run forward, not sure whether to be afraid or maybe she just found something cool. The right choice was fear. About thirty feet in front of her is a mountain lion! I instinctively stand in front of Angel-Girl, shielding her body, pressing her with one hand close to my back. We have spotted mountain lion tracks over the years but I have never seen one in Sedona or ever met anyone that's spotted one.

"Don't move, baby," I say, keeping my voice very quiet and calm.

The mountain lion is young, not a full-grown adult. She just stands still, peering at us. If fear-bolts weren't racing through me, I would think how incredibly beautiful she is – those luminescent green eyes and the luster of her golden fur! I feel Angel-Girl's wriggling behind me. I steal a quick glance down at the ground and can see she has squatted down between my legs so she can see the mountain lion.

"Don't move, baby, please." I whisper, imploring her, trying to keep the alarm out of my voice.

Then the wildest thing happens after she lowers herself. The mountain lion sits back on her haunches, lowering her head slightly, appearing to stare right at my daughter!

"Daddy, did you see that?" Angel-Girl whispers.

"Yes," I reply, a little blown away.

As I stand there, I am rapidly trying to process what the next best move is to keep my daughter safe. I know running in these situations is the worst thing you can do. There is an old Shamanic Toltec maneuver I could use, putting Angel-Girl on my shoulders to make us appear enormous as way of scaring the lion. Or I could just start yelling and waving my arms. I scan the ground around me to see if there is a substantial branch I could grab to ward her off, in case she attacks – but there's not even a twig. As the mountain lion continues to sit on her haunches, it makes me quiet my own thinking for a moment. Something inside tells me to just be still.

I'm taken back to an event many years ago when I was with Holy Men on a hike and we ran into a grizzly bear. They stood unfazed, while I was quietly freaking out. The bear was about fifty feet away. My brothers stood very still, breathing deeply, each with his whole body. I had been with them for enough years to know to follow their lead and to trust them. The bear suddenly stood up on his hind legs and roared at us, jaws fully open and teeth bared. The intensity of its ferociousness pierced every part of my body. I could feel my legs shaking. My brothers did not move. They just kept peering at the bear with deep focus and continued the full-body breathing I had seen when they were shape-shifting.

In my shamanism, one of my predilections is my deep relationship and partnership with animal totems. Over thirty years ago, I met my panther and it was this special friendship that opened the door to the shamanic world. He is my brother, we are as one. His fierceness of spirit, his allegiance has helped me through so much over the years. The Holy Men recognized my totem connection right away and passed on to me their ancestral knowledge of shape-shifting and how to nurture a relationship with one's totems. I've found that my panther is able to see into the darkness of my clients' emotions. He can identify their blocks, which are keeping them from moving forward towards healing or their own wisdom. Panthers, of course, see in the dark!

After a long moment, the bear dropped back down on all fours and walked slowly off. The Holy Men raised their hands in a formal goodbye and we moved on through the trees. I knew to not ask them right away about what had transpired – the need to know everything immediately is always a mistake with them! The next day I felt it was the right moment to ask them about our encounter with the bear. They said quietly, "We were feeling the bear's heart." I took a long moment to absorb that, feeling the sacredness of their act. Then I asked them what would have happened if the bear had attacked. They gazed directly in my eyes, and responded in the serious warrior tone I had come to know, "Hoka-hey, brother, Hoka-hey," which loosely translates to mean, "Today is a good day to die." I responded, honoring their wisdom with "A Ho."

Bringing myself quickly back to the present, I peer closely across the space between Angel-Girl and me and the mountain lion, who is breathing with her whole body as cats do.

"Baby, can you see how deeply she is breathing?" I say, very quietly.

"Yes! I am breathing with her," she says.

"You are?"

"Like you taught me."

What she is doing is the first step in connecting with her animal totem – to breathe in rhythm with it. The most powerful form of communication is always non-verbal.

But she is doing it with a *real live mountain lion*, not an animal totem who resides in the dreamweave (alternative universe)! She must have actually been listening when I told her about the Holy Men and the grizzly for one of her bedtime stories. She is a giant sponge when it comes to anything about shamanism. I did leave out the part about Hoka-hey because I felt she was too young to hear that.

I begin to breathe in rhythm with my daughter and the lion, letting my eyes go very soft and gentle as I gaze into the lion's eyes – just projecting *connection*. I sense how all the sounds around us hush, and the branches of the trees seem to go still. After a minute, the mountain lion gets up on all fours and then does something strange – she presses her front left paw into the soft red earth. At least that's what I think I see her do – or am I just imagining it? She lowers her head, peering underneath me at Angel-Girl. I sense no danger in the mountain lion's body energy or in her expression – how I know this, I'm not sure.

I continue to hear Angel-Girl breathing deeply, slowly. And then the mountain lion turns and scurries into the trees. I notice she is limping a little as she disappears over the crest of a hill.

"Daddy, did you see!"

"Yes, my Angel, I did – she's limping."

"It's my mountain lion!"

"I think you are right." She is referring to the hike we took a year ago where we found a mountain lion track and then Angel had a "seeing vision" of that mountain lion limping.

Angel-Girl stands up, eyes wide, appearing a little stunned or out of it. Her demeanor or expression feels familiar to me but I can't quite identify it.

"Cool!" she exclaims about our encounter.

"Cool is right!"

She walks over to where the mountain lion was standing and examines the earth closely.

"Daddy, look! She left her paw print, just like the one I found before. Wow!" She points down at a very defined paw print in the red soil. It's bigger than you'd think it would be.

"Yup, it looks like she did! Maybe she's talking to you." I wonder to myself, *She left her print? Is that possible?* As I scan the trees to make sure we're safe, I'm caught between wanting to explore this with my daughter and trying to create some fast-distance between us and the mountain lion, wherever she might be. I'm not sure Angel-Girl gets how much danger we were just in.

Angel-Girl kneels down on the ground and puts her little hand over the print.

"What do you think she is trying to tell me?" she asks.

"What do you feel, baby?"

She presses her hand deeper into the paw print and closes her eyes again.

"I see her, like before! She is looking at me!"

"Awesome."

"I like her a lot. Maybe she's lonely out here."

"Baby, we have to remember she can be dangerous

and we have to be very careful. Okay?"

There is something about this that doesn't make her happy but she replies, "Okay."

"Let's head back and we can talk about in on the way. You lead!" I have her lead on purpose so that in case our friend comes back behind us, I will be between her and Angel-Girl.

We walk out of the magical forest, Angel's excitement bouncing off the Tree-People on either side of the trail, as she asks me question after question as only an apprentice-shaman-in-training would do who just met a mountain lion!

That night I tuck her into bed after she tells all her bears about her big meeting with the mountain lion and how she breathed with the lion and the lion left her print for her.

A few hours later, I settle into bed, feeling unusually quiet inside myself. I'm not sure if it's from the danger of what happened or the mysterious quality of it. Suddenly, I hear a sound in the house that is out of place. I sit up and go completely still, trying to identify it and where it's emanating from. When I realize it's coming from Angel-Girl's room, I get out of bed and head for her door. As I get close, I hear *growling!* The hair on every part of my body stands straight up and fear rushes through me. I open her door quickly and see her sound asleep in her bed. But I distinctly hear her growling! It's very real-sounding; if I close my eyes I'm positive I would think there was an animal in the room.

I have an immediate suspicion about what's happening so I don't wake her. The answer to what the mountain lion was trying to tell her is happening. I squat down on my haunches by the door to watch her. This lowering myself to my haunches is actually purposeful. I witnessed my brothers, the Holy Men, do this dozens of times in moments that were important in some way to my journey – some crossroads moment where I went deeper into my Spirit. I felt supported when they lowered themselves in this position – it was like saying, *We are not going anywhere.* I do this with clients or Angel-Girl in their important crossroads. It's also my way to connect with the Holy Men and their energy.

I go very still inside and I observe Angel-Girl with each passing moment get more restless and as her growling gets louder and more ferocious, her breathing becomes more rapid.

Suddenly, she sits up like a shot, eyes opening in alarm; she starts panting, one breath coming quickly after another. She sees me watching her but can't seem to speak.

I give her ten seconds and then say, "You turned into a mountain lion in your dream, didn't you?" I ask her this rhetorically as way to get her grounded. It's also my way of saying, *There's nothing to be afraid of, I know what's going on.*

She nods her head vigorously, her eyes wild.

"She's still inside you?" I ask, keeping my matter-of-fact tone.

She nods again, her face reflecting a little nervousness and not sure what to do.

"It's okay, baby. Take some long, deep breaths, through your nose and out of your mouth. Watch me."

I breathe to show her and she matches my breathing rhythm – getting more centered and calmer with each breath.

"Good girl. Now, say this for me – from your heart as always, 'I ask the mountain lion to please separate from me. Thank you for joining with me. My heart is full. We are one body, two breaths. A Ho, thank you for honoring me.'"

She repeats everything I say, word for word, the sincerity that always flows from her in every phrase. Her body shudders a little at the end of her words – this is the mountain lion separating from her.

"Now, my Angel, say, 'My emotional, spiritual, and mental body are deeply connected to my physical body and my physical body is deeply rooted in the womb of Mother Earth,' Really feel that, honey."

Again, she repeats everything I say, putting full intention into each word, sensing her body and its connection to the Earth.

"Now say this, 'All my personal energy is back inside myself.'"

I give her a long moment to let these invocations set in.

"You feel better?" I ask, lightening my voice to let her know she has passed through the experience.

She grins with her usual Angel-Girl-coziness and nods her head again, as if she's not yet ready to speak to me. Then her attention is caught by something and she blurts out, "Daddy! The mountain lion is sitting right there, looking at me!" She points excitedly to the foot of her bed.

I look where is she is pointing and with my clairvoyance I can see the beautiful mountain lion with her green eyes watching over my daughter, a protective energy flowing from her. When they show up like this it means they have *joined* you. It's a major moment on the shamanic path to be joined with your animal totem. It's as if the Old Ones are saying you are truly ready.

I raise my hand in formal greeting. "I say, A Ho, to my daughter and her mountain lion!"

"Is it *my* totem, Daddy?" she whispers across to me, eyes wide, not quite believing it's possible.

I nod my head quickly and purposefully as the Holy Men would do for me to confirm an important question. Then, with ceremonious pride, I say, "It is so, sister to the mountain lion. It is so."

Chapter Thirteen

Golden-Bear
(Angel-Girl at eight years old)

It's Friday evening and I am cleaning up in the kitchen and, as always, blessing the inventor of the dishwasher! But somebody called Angel-Girl should be helping me!

I call out to my eight year old daughter, "Hey! You there?"

"I'm in the laundry room."

"You're in the laundry room?"

"Definitely! Doing laundry!" I hear some muffled giggling.

She doesn't help with the laundry – yet! Just "helps" in making her clothes as dirty as possible in the red Sedona dirt.

"What are you really doing in there?" I hear a cabinet door close suddenly.

"Nothing." I'm suspicious but let it go.

"Last time, I checked the chore-list, Angel-Girl should be helping her very cool father with the dishes!"

"Angel-Girl only has ca-ca father, not cool one!"

"Is that so! Okay…Hmmm…Isn't it time for the monthly trip to Flag…"

Before I finish the last syllable, she bursts into the kitchen, her eyes bright with excitement. "When are we going? Are we going to the bookstore?" She bounces up and down, impatient for an answer.

I put on my best insulted face, "Well, I was going tomorrow afternoon but weren't you the Angel-Girl that just announced she doesn't have a cool father? That was you, right?"

"No, Daddy! You are the coolest of all daddies."

"Uh huh!"

"There is no daddy as cool as you in Sedona!"

"Just Sedona?"

"The whole world!"

"The whole world? Hmmm…" I stand there, pretending to consider her fate. "Okay, you can go!"

"Yaaayyyy!" she says, hugging me.

"But someone has chores first, correct?"

"Yes, definitely!"

She loves Bookman's in Flagstaff, which is a super-large used bookstore. Northern Arizona University is around the corner, so a lot of books flow into the place. It's bigger than most Barnes & Nobles. They have a huge children's book section – tens of thousands of books and videos for kids four to twelve in age. All are very cheap, so we usually leave with a box of books for very little money. Angel-Girl goes crazy in the place! She loves to read. She loves to *find* books. The teachers report to me she reads three grade levels above her age group. On weekends, she will spend hours in her room reading. I have to drag her out to eat! The first time we went to Bookman's and I guided her back to the kids' section, she stood frozen, scanning the shelves and shelves of books, then peered up at me with eyes as big as saucers – like this couldn't be possible. She was in heaven. I told her she could pick ten books.

"Really?" she asked. "We can take them home and they are mine?"

I nodded, so happy to see her excited.

Back in the kitchen, she asks, "What's my budget at the bookstore?"

I laugh. "Your budget? Where did you learn that word?"

"I looked it up!"

"Excellent. Well, how many books and videos are you selling back?"

"No, Daddy, please, they are very cozy in my room!"

I shake my head in disbelief. "No, you're not wearing me down this time. How many books are you returning?"

"I only have twelve books in my room!"

I can't help but laugh. "twelve books! I think it's more like 100!"

"I can't count that high, Daddy."

"Uh huh! After you do your chores, you'll have to find four books you can part with."

"Four?" she whines.

"Yes, four," I say lightly but firmly so she knows I mean it.

As we work together to clean up the kitchen, putting

dishes in the dishwasher and wiping down the counter, I think about her need to keep books. I first began to understand why when I brought her to the library, thinking she might like the children's section and after fifteen minutes she told me she couldn't find anything. I was stunned. I asked her why and she just shrugged her shoulders, so I didn't push it. But on the drive home, she was very quiet so I asked her again why she didn't take anything. She said sadly, "You can't keep them, Daddy." Then I got it. It's like she is getting this beautiful thing, a book, which she gets such immense pleasure from and then she has to give it back to the library. After the death of her mom, she wants to hold onto what she loves. She has lost enough.

After Angel-Girl finishes her kitchen chores, she goes to her room and comes back carrying just one book.

"I only have one," she says. "Golden-Bear says he wants to read the other three I picked.

"You're killing me!"

"I'm serious, Daddy, come look."

We go across the hall to her bedroom and sitting on the floor next her bookcase is Golden-Bear, a beautiful golden teddy bear, leaning over three stacked books as if he's holding them down with his paws. He is a very important member of our family.

I glance down at Angel-Girl and she shrugs her shoulders like it's not her fault

"Some of the bears like to hear all the stories again," she says. "We don't want to be unprepared."

"Four books, little mountain lion. Understood?"

She gives up. "Yes, Daddy."

When I get to her door, I turn back and say, "Golden-Bear can keep two of those three!"

She runs up and almost knocks me down as she hugs me, "Thank you, thank you!"

"Okay, baby," I say happily. "You brought Golden-Bear into it! You're very sneaky."

"He loves those books, Daddy. They are about bears that were found like him."

Golden-Bear and I found each other one lonely night twenty-three years ago when I was on a business road-trip in the middle of a little town in Pennsylvania. On top of my teaching and healing work back in those days, I also published art prints by Native American artists and sold Native American hand-painted drums. So I traveled on the road every few weeks to art galleries and Native American shops on the eastern seaboard. In that moment of time, I was going through a really rough period with my elderly mom who had multiple health issues, including severe emphysema. The rest of my family had passed by that time, including my older brother, so everything was left up to me and I was feeling pretty alone in the world. My mom was recovering from minor surgery in the hospital and because of a loss of oxygen to the brain from the COPD, she started hallucinating badly: she literally didn't recognize me. The psychiatrist at the hospital had no idea how to handle it. I made some calls and discovered the top geriatric psychiatric hospital in the country was only a half-hour away: NYU at Cornell. Then I had to do what no son should be faced with – I had to petition to have my mother committed to a psychiatric hospital.

I can vividly remember standing with my family doctor of thirty years in the hospital hallway, both of us with tears in our eyes as the nurses wheeled my mom down the hall to be transferred. I was a wreck. The day after I signed those commitment papers, I had an appointment in Pennsylvania with a gallery owner. I could not cancel. Bills were mounting. On the way, a New Jersey State trooper pulled me over for speeding. I was still pretty emotional and drained. I remember apologizing and telling him exactly what had happened with my mom, and actually handed him the admitting papers, which I still had in the car. He was very kind and let me go.

The appointment with the gallery owner was for 7:00 pm in a homey arts-and-crafts village. It was dark when I arrived and the gallery employee told me the owner was expecting me and would return in fifteen minutes. I decided to wander around, something I didn't usually do on these selling trips. But it had been a long, lonely drive and I just felt the need to settle my Spirit. I noticed a small crafts shop across the street and felt a very tangible pull to go in. So I crossed the street and as I walked through the front door, I heard above me a beautiful tinkling of a bell; it sounded different than most other door bells – fairy-like! The store was empty except for a dark-haired woman in her early fifties behind the counter. I noticed her friendly eyes right away. But she seemed pretty focused and serious about some paperwork in front of her; it appeared to be end-of-the-day bookkeeping.

"Hi!" I said and smiled.

"Hi!" She responded, as her smile lit up her face, transforming her.

"Are you closing up?"

"No, not yet."

I glanced around the shop. "Okay if I look around?"

"Of course!" I felt embraced by her welcoming energy.

"Thank you."

I turned down the first aisle, studying different handmade toys and jewel boxes, just a whole assortment of lovely things. Suddenly, my attention was pulled to the right and there, sitting on an upper-shelf, was the *happiest-looking* golden teddy bear I had ever seen. He was about fourteen inches high, sitting, with a red and green Christmas bow around his neck. I couldn't take my eyes off him. My whole Spirit went deeply quiet and time seemed to slow down. Something was vibrating in that little shop. I just immediately felt like this little golden bear and I knew each other. His loving expression, his kind energy was like a much-needed hug. I have no idea how long I stood there. I reached out and brushed his golden fur with my hand; it was so soft, it felt like home. Scanning around, I noticed he was the only teddy bear in the shop. *That's strange*, I thought to myself. I wondered how much he was and found the price tag. Expensive. I was struggling then, trying to support myself and my mom, so I felt as if I couldn't spend the money – things were really tight. My heart sank a little. But I didn't feel like I could move from that spot. The room grew very still. Then something occurred to me.

I approached the owner, "Hi. That's a very special bear."

She smiled, "Yes, he certainly is." I sensed she believed it, and wasn't just agreeing with the customer.

"I'm in town meeting the gallery owner across the street. I publish Native American art prints."

"Oh, wonderful. The owner is very nice." There was just an innate friendliness about this woman.

I hesitated, and then said, "I was wondering…" I pulled back again for a second, fearful of what she would say to what I was about to propose. "Would you possibly consider trading that special bear for one of my prints?" I could feel the nervousness in my voice. "I have a signed and numbered wolf print you might really like that's valued at $75."

Right away, she said, "I'd love to see it."

I was really surprised. "Great! I'll be right back!"

I hurried out, ran across the street, drove my jeep over to her shop and parked, getting the 16" x 15" wolf print out of the back. I carried it gently into the store and handed it to her.

"It's beautiful!" she said. "What's it's called?"

"*The Unseen Wolf.*"

"I love that!"

"I'm glad!" I responded, sensing her considering the trade. I looked directly in her eyes and said, "It would really mean a lot to me." I hoped she could hear in my voice and see in my eyes how important this was to me.

She said, "Okay, let's do it!"

"Really? Wow! Thank you so much." I was stunned. "May I take him down?"

She nodded, a big smile on her face, as if she appreciated the formality of my question.

I gently took the teddy bear off the shelf; I could feel him smiling at me and I held him securely against my chest as I walked back to the owner. "Thank you," I said, choking up a little.

I saw her notice how I was holding him, and I knew she understood.

"Thank you for the print!"

"My pleasure."

"Come back again!"

"Take care."

Of all the bears that Angel-Girl and I have, he is the only one I found myself, all the others were gifted to me. I felt so blessed as I walked out to the jeep with him and when we got in, I gave him a big, long hug and whispered, "Thank you for finding me." He was so soft! I could feel the pain around my mom ease – like a voice saying, "It's going to be okay." I put him carefully on the passenger seat, tucking a sweater around him so he would be warm. His name flowed instantly up in me: Golden-Bear! He and I have traveled a lot of miles together in the jeep. I go, he goes. I know deep in my heart he was a gift from the Old Ones when I really needed a friend. Things began to get better soon after I found him. Three weeks later, my mom walked out of the psychiatric hospital, completely fine. When Shyheart came into my life and she was low or sick, she used to sleep with Golden-Bear, holding him very close. I would get into bed next to them and hold them both tightly against me.

My relationship with all the bears that live with us is about my shamanism where everything in my world is alive. I have a theory that little angels inhabit stuffed animals. I've had several guests or clients in the house who have commented, "There is something that goes on with these stuffed animals here."

"What do you mean?" I ask.

"Don't know how to explain it, it's like they have energy."

If you honor them, they will honor you.

The next day, Angel-Girl and I are on our way to Flagstaff, which is an hour away on 89A. It's truly one of the most beautiful drives in the country. The trees have a way of closing over the road creating a canopy; it's like driving through a lush green tunnel.

I see Angel-Girl in the mirror, buzzing in the back seat, anxious to get up the mountain to the bookstore. She's been telling me about latest happenings at school.

When we get to top of the switchbacks and are about fifteen minutes from Flagstaff, I ask her, "And you didn't want to bring Golden-Bear?"

"No, Daddy, he is happy at home, he told me which books he would like."

"Okay."

Back at the house before we left, I made a point to ask her if she wanted to bring him. I did this purposely because of something that happened on a trip to the bookstore about four months ago when Golden-Bear was with us; she likes to bring him sometimes on our different adventures, just like I used too. We had spent about an hour in the bookstore and as we were checking out, I glanced down at Angel-Girl and suddenly noticed something was missing.

"Where's Golden-Bear?" I yelled in alarm. A little too aggressively, an anger rushing up in me.

My daughter looked up at me, terrified, and bolted back to the children's section. Fifteen seconds later, she came back, holding Golden-Bear tightly against her chest. As she walked over to me, she was on the verge of tears. "I'm sorry, Daddy."

"It's okay, honey," I said, stroking her hair, forcing myself to be calm.

I quickly paid the bill and started to walk out, holding her hand, sensing her glancing up at me, a look of fear on her face. I have never seen her this afraid. It made me feel horrible. Why had I overreacted with such anger? As soon as we got outside in the fresh air, I could feel myself start breathing again. I hadn't even realized I had stopped. We got to the Explorer and she was still watching me, so I smiled, trying to communicate to her that everything was okay. She was clutching Golden-Bear like her life depended on it. I lifted them up into her car seat and she yelled with a sob, "I am so sorry, Daddy, please don't be mad at me."

My heart broke. I lowered myself to her height so she could see my face.

"It's okay, my Angel. I am really sorry I reacted that way. Please forgive me."

"I didn't mean to let go of Golden-Bear." She was crying hard, the tears spilling over his golden fur.

I tried to capture her full attention with the *warrior voice* she knows; speaking with total conviction and deep caring.

"Listen to me, okay?" I waited for her to acknowledge me. When she nodded, the tears slowing, I continued, "You have taken Golden-Bear hundreds of places, right?"

She reluctantly nodded her head.

"Have you ever forgotten him?"

"No," she said, calming a little.

"That's right. There is no one and I mean *no one* that I trust more than you with the bears…no one. I am so proud of you and how you take care of them and watch over them. You are an impeccable warrior." Even at eight years old, she knows what the word *impeccable* means and its importance in the culture of the warrior. She understands it's the highest compliment I could give her.

I felt the fierce emotion that came from living the life I have lived flow up in me. I hoped my eyes were shining with it as I peered deeply into my daughter's blue eyes and asked firmly, "A Ho?" – the warrior's acknowledgment of pure truth. I could see from her sudden focus that she was hearing me and feeling me, and understood I was very serious.

"A Ho," she responded, her voice stronger.

"Good. I am really sorry for my bad voice back there." I hesitated a moment, trying to understand my own actions. "I think the anger about your losing your mom just shot up in me in that moment because I was afraid I lost someone else. It was just a split second and it frightened me and it turned to anger. Does that make sense?"

She nodded her head up and down.

"You sure?"

"I felt that too, Daddy." She started to cry again. And I brought her into my arms.

"I am so sorry," I said. "We're both scared of losing anyone else. That makes sense, baby. But we're okay, we have Golden-Bear and each other. Nothing is going to happen to us."

She has not brought Golden-Bear back to the store since then but I am not going to force it; an insight will come to me about how to make her feel it's safe to carry him with her. I deeply regret losing my cool that day and have had a tough time forgiving myself. But I realize that I have to, so that *she* will forgive herself.

Four months later as we turn off the interstate, I turn to her and say, "Okay, now remember, when we get to the parking lot, don't leap out of the car like a wild banshee. I don't want you to get killed running across the parking lot!"

"What's a banshee?"

"Angel-Girl on a book-hunt!"

"Okay." I look in the rearview and see that she's trying to suppress a smile.

"I mean it!"

"OKAY!"

"What?"

"Sorry."

We exchange grins in the mirror.

"Maybe Melissa will be there today?" Angel-Girl asks.

"Maybe…" I say.

Melissa is her special friend at the bookstore who watches over the children's book section. She shows Angel-Girl all the books she thinks she will like. I don't give away that I actually called to make sure Melissa would be working today – my daughter is not the only sneaky one in the family!

"What's my budget, Daddy? She will want to know."

"I was thinking $25."

"Wow! Really! I can probably get fifteen books for that – maybe more!"

"You've been an excellent helper."

"Cool!"

We pull into the parking lot and I watch her in the mirror and just laugh to myself; her blues eyes are sparkling with excitement. I wish I still felt that way, and then I remind myself that I do – about my daughter!

I hop out, go around the truck, and she grabs my hand.

"Don't run," I say and she actually seems to listen to me. She walks slowly, very composed. I think to myself, *I guess I'm getting this parenting stuff down!* We move through the front door and as soon as we hit the carpet of the store, she tears away from me and runs, pretty much like a wild banshee, across the store to the children's section. So much for my parenting!

This is maybe our twentieth trip here in the last three years and she knows everyone in the store by name! She runs past the check-out counter and calls out to a tall young twenty-something-guy with a pony tail sporting a tied-dyed shirt and bellbottom jeans, "Hi Mike!"

"Hi Angel!"

Then, she says, "Hi Sam!" to a fiftyish, studious-looking man, wearing horn-rimmed glasses with "Manager" on his name plate.

He brightens when he sees her, "Hey Angel!"

She runs into the children's section and sees her buddy. "Melissa!"

"Hi Angel!" Melissa is an incredibly sweet girl in her late twenties; she's brunette, thin, and I can tell by her dark eyes she has seen some rough times. In the middle of a conversation, she sometimes catches me off-guard by suddenly smiling for no reason. If I was twenty-five years younger, I'd be asking her out!

"My dad said I have a budget of $25!" Angel-Girl blurts out, not able to get the words out fast enough.

"Fantastic! I saved you a lot of books, especially the one you requested about mountain lions."

"Really?"

"And…" She leans in, whispering in Angel-Girl's ear and catches my eye as I stand at the entrance to the children's section. I wave, nod, turning over the steering wheel to her.

Angel-Girl whispers back. I wonder what that is all about. She's just like a little mountain lion—sneaky! Melissa leads her over to a cardboard box that has Angel's name handwritten on the side in beautiful calligraphy.

"Here's your special box!" I knew that Melissa saves books for Angel-Girl but the box is a new thing.

My daughter's eyes go big. "*My* box?"

"When a book comes in that I think you will like, I put it in here so no one but you will see it. I only do this for my special customers."

"Wow," she says awed.

Melissa sits down cross-legged on the floor in front of the box and Angel-Girl joins her, looks at the box, and then back up at Melissa; she is sort of nervous and not sure what to do.

"Go ahead, check them out," Melissa says.

She peers into the box, as if there is precious treasure waiting for her, and then very carefully takes out the top book, laying it gently in her lap.

"Oh, that's my favorite!" Melissa exclaims.

Angel-Girl moves her head up and down rapidly, her tiny frame literally vibrating with joy.

Melissa glances over at me. I raise my palm and mouth silently, "Thank you." She smiles and nods to say it's her pleasure. It's so obvious how much this young woman loves what she does.

I get a kick out of watching my daughter go on her hunt and seeing the wonder and passion that springs up in her face but I don't want her to feel like I'm hovering. This is her time. And I totally trust she will be safe here with Melissa.

"Angel, I am going to be over in the fiction section if you need me."

"Okay, Dad," she says, totally immersed in her book, not even looking up. I laugh. I am suddenly "Dad" not "Daddy."

An hour later, we are walking out to the car with a box of books. It looks like she has about twenty!

"What kind of books did you get today?"

"Lots of cool ones! Melissa saved them for me."

"That's awesome. What were you two whispering about back there?"

"Secret stuff!"

"Okay. How about pizza?"

"Yayyy, pizza!" On the way back to Sedona, Angel-Girl conks out and sleeps all the way home. I carry her into her bedroom from the car, laying her gently down, and then I retrieve her box of books from the back seat because I know she won't sleep unless they're in the room with her. I help my daughter get into her pjs and tuck her in, giving her Golden-Bear, whom she immediately hugs tightly.

I lean down and kiss her. "Goodnight, my Angel. I love you very much." I kiss Golden-Bear, too. "Goodnight, buddy. I love you, too. Sleep tight."

"Goodnight, Daddy," Angel-Girl says drowsily. "Thank you for my books. I love you."

I check that her night-light is glowing and just before turning off the overhead light, I notice that her bookcase doesn't have anywhere near 100 books – but there are certainly more than twelve! Well, I think, *I guess I miscalculated.*

I close her door until there is just a crack remaining and then I head to the kitchen to make some tea. Waiting for the water to boil, I'm puzzled by something that stirs in my memory: *What was she doing in the laundry room yesterday?*

I wander into the laundry room, turn on the light, and scan the room trying to discern what the little lion could be up to in here. One lower cabinet door is slightly open. I very seldom go into these cabinets, maybe once a month, if that. I swing the door open, but I don't see anything unusual, just stuff we are storing in there: candles, old tools, videocassettes, dated telephone books. When I go to close the door the glint of something shiny catches my eye; whatever it is, it's tucked way in the back corner of the cabinet, as if it's been carefully hidden from view.

Reaching blindly in, I feel a box with some paper covering it so I slowly lift it out into the light. It's a box wrapped in yellow-metallic paper that hasn't been taped yet. I remember using this paper for one of Angel-Girl's birthday presents. *What is this?* I wonder. I sit down cross-legged on the floor, with the box on my lap, and notice there is a mailing label on the top that looks to be in her handwriting. I can't make out what it says so I jump up, run to my office, find my reading glasses, and return. Sitting back on the floor, I read the label: St. Jude Children's Hospital, 262 Danny Thomas Place, Memphis, TN 38105. For the return address, she has written: Angel & Golden-Bear Drambour, with our address. What is she sending? I am anxious to see what's inside so I gently unwrap the pretty yellow paper and lift off the top lid of the box. "Oh, man…you're kidding me," I say aloud. "Wow." I feel the tears coming. Inside the box are two dozen children's books. I look closer and see the two on top are the books that Golden-Bear was holding yesterday and then the next five are about sick kids getting better, books I have never seen on her shelf. That's what she and Melissa were whispering about. Secret stuff.

I pat the books gently, lovingly, and whisper through my tears, through my swelling heart, "Thank you, thank you."

Chapter Fourteen

Fred
(Angel-Girl at eight years old)

Every fifteen minutes for the past hour I see a blur run by my study door. Of course, this blur is Angel-Girl. She is breaking the "no-running-in-the-house" rule but I just let it go today; I am having a great writing day and the creative muse is in full force so I am feeling flexible with the rules! As she makes another pass, I yell out, teasing her, "I guess that running back and forth means you're ready to go get your hair cut?" Her wavy brunette hair has gotten really out of control – it's sticking out in every direction and covers her face; it's like peering through a veil to see her blue eyes.

These periodic haircuts are traumatic ordeals for her, to the point she barricades herself under her bed, using all her stuffed animals as shields! I have a suspicion why it's so emotional but any gentle probing is met with a wall. So I am attempting the "keeping-it-light-approach!" I don't mind personally that her hair is unruly, but I've begun to get disapproving looks from her third-grade teacher whenever I pick Angel-Girl up from school, and I think this is the reason why.

My daughter yells an emphatic "No!" from the other room and I laugh to think that playfully teasing her was going to have any effect.

Finally, I go to investigate and see she is gazing out the living room window into the front yard, which is in full summer bloom with a variety of lavender sage bushes, pink and red flowering crate myrtle bushes, a maple tree, agaves, and a globe willow that is very special to me.

"Angel-Girl, what are you doing out here?" I ask.

"I'm checking on Fred, Dad," she says, as if this is the most obvious thing in the world, and then she returns to looking out the window with a studied gaze.

"Who's Fred?"

Keeping her eyes focused outside, she says to me over her shoulder, "The big tree that you and Mr. Roberto moved from the backyard to the front."

She is referring to an eight-foot Arizona Cyprus we transplanted to get better sun. The tree was looking pretty scraggly, and our landscaper, whom Angel-Girl refers to as "Mr. Roberto," felt it needed a new home. Angel-Girl has turned into Roberto's assistant and she eagerly helps him out whenever he's working on the property. I have attempted to stop her so Roberto can focus on his work but I am just no match for her passion to take care of plants and trees! And Roberto seems to really appreciate the assistance and company. They never stop chatting to each other as they work and I admire her deep listening when

Roberto is explaining planting techniques. I have a suspicion that Roberto has adjusted his schedule so he is here when she is. I am super-proud of Angel-Girl's work ethic. I bought her a little shovel and other miniature tools so she can dig along with him. After the first few times, I handed her $16 for two hours of work. She looked baffled and said, "Daddy, I am taking care of the Plant-People and Tree-People, you don't need to pay me for that!" I wanted her to know the importance of being compensated for her work, but her conviction persuades me to just let it be.

I respond to the new name, "Oh, I didn't know that you called the tree Fred."

Turning to me she says, "Yes, definitely! I asked him and he said that was his name."

"Good enough for me! Fred it is! Are you afraid Fred will fall?"

"No, I saw that you and Mr. Roberto made sure he was safe with all those ropes."

"Well, it was more Mr. Roberto than me."

"I saw you talking to Fred and that helps too." I notice she keeps turning back and forth from me to Fred, never letting her attention on him falter for too long.

"So what's wrong, sweetie?"

"I just think it's important to check on him until he gets used to his new home." Her sensitivity to unspoken needs is so amazing – for people, trees, stuffed animals, even my car! Her mother, Shyheart, embodied this quality; she just had a way of knowing what you needed and when you needed it. I try to teach couples the importance of this – it has a powerful way of enriching relationships – *what is it that my partner needs right now?*

"Is that why you keep running back and forth?"

She nods her head vigorously, keeping her attention on Fred.

"That's really nice of you." I think a moment and then ask, "Should we go outside and say hello to Fred?"

"I am outside, Daddy," she responds off-handedly.

Her words stun me. "You mean, you are *seeing* yourself outside with Fred right now?"

"Yes, like you taught me. I am standing next to him, patting him." She glances back at me with a big smile to show me how happy this makes her.

I've only explained to her how to do this *once*. She is projecting herself, an advanced shamanic tool I use sometimes with clients – and I mean, *advanced*. I stand observing her, blown away by how quickly she has absorbed and implemented this technique of seeing herself in another location. It usually takes lots of years of practice for someone to be effective at this. I use it for a variety of reasons, but mostly for physical or energetic healing and clearing when I sense a client has lots of shields up. If I feel a lot of resistance from them, I will project myself close to them or even project one of my animal totems and then I am able to get under their energetic radar so to speak.

"Angel-Girl, why did you decide to visit with Fred this way?" I inquire.

"I'm not sure, it just *felt* better this way." She pats her chest to show me where she felt it.

"Good girl!" She gives me a huge grin and returns to visiting with Fred. Her decision to project herself came from a *feeling*, an inspiration. And she simply followed her feelings, like I try to model to her. It's one of the principles of the code of the warrior that I have been teaching her. I call it "No-Gap," which means there should be no distance between hearing a spiritual whisper or insight and immediately acting on it. And more importantly, not asking *why* Spirit wants you to do something, which is a way of honoring the dictates of Spirit with faith.

After a long minute, Angel-Girl turns to me and says, "Okay, Dad, I'm done! Fred says he is making friends with the protectors."

"The agaves?"

"Yup!" she exclaims, excited about them connecting.

It's my instinct that agave plants with their spiny and pointy, thick leaves are guardians over special or sacred places. They stand vigil over many of the places of power to which I guide clients. I am deeply honored to have six of them in the front yard protecting the house.

"Fred says he feels much better in the front of the house," she reports to me with a sense of relief.

"That's awesome! Did he tell you why?"

"He likes people and he enjoys seeing them driving by. He says that not all of them speak to Tree-People but definitely some do!" I see her pondering for a moment. "You teach your clients how to talk to trees, right, Daddy?"

"For sure, most of them love it."

"Are there more trees than people?" she asks with that beautiful innocence only children seem to display.

"Wow, that's a great question! I would say, probably." I watch her give this some thought, then she says, "Well, if people talked to all the Tree-People then they would have lots and lots of friends and they wouldn't be sad!!"

"That's a wonderful way to look at it."

She turns her attention back out the window towards Fred.

"People get lonely, don't they? Like your clients?" she asks, not wanting anyone to feel bad. It's both wonderful and hard for me sometimes to witness her caring so much. I don't want her to be heavy-hearted.

"Yes, they do, my daughter, yes they do." For a moment, the faces of some of my clients flash inside my thoughts.

"I can feel it," she says, looking disappointed. Then she asks, "Some people don't have daddies or mommies who tell them it's okay to talk to the Tree-People, do they?"

Reluctantly, I shake my head no.

She comes over to where I am standing and hugs me tight and says, "Thank you, Daddy, for teaching me." Wow, I think. What do you say to that, brothers and sisters?

I hug her back, my voice husky. "You got it, baby,"

"Daddy…?" She pulls away so she can see my face. By

her tone, I can sense she's apprehensive about telling me something.

"What, honey?" I say softly, stroking her hair.

"I hate getting my hair cut," she says to me in a very serious, adult tone. I can really feel the pain in her words. Her eyes start to well up.

I keep my eyes totally focused on her and simply nod my head up and down in understanding, hoping my expression reflects that I am truly absorbing the importance of her message. I ask her gently, "Can you share with me why, my Angel?"

She stares at me for a long moment, I think trying to gauge if she can voice the words. Finally, making an effort to hold back tears, she says, "Because, mommy's hair was long and it makes me feel closer to her." This is what I surmised.

I am not sure if it's the mention of her mother's hair or how awed I am by her courage to verbalize this, but everything inside me goes silent and very still. Again, I just nod my head, communicating with all my energy, *I totally get it, my daughter.*

"You understand, right, Daddy?" The vulnerability in her voice pierces through a door inside me that I didn't know was closed.

"You bet I do, baby. We'll figure it out."

"Thank you, Daddy." She squeezes me with her little arms.

I peer over her head out the window and notice Fred's

long branches swaying in the breeze, then I register with my "seeing" that he's feeling us – how wonderful! Suddenly, I sense a warm presence surrounding us.

Then, right away, Angel-Girl announces happily, "Daddy, Fred is hugging us. Cool! I feel better."

If you honor them, they will honor you.

Chapter Fifteen

The Monsters!
(Angel-Girl at eight years old)

Tonight, after I tuck Angel-Girl in, I decide to head to bed early and read. Ever since I was a kid I have loved reading. I was forced to go to boarding schools for seven years and in those unwelcoming places I found a sanctuary within books.

My bedroom always gentles my soul. The minute I walk into the room, full of maple wood and soft blue colors, I relax; blue helps me feel my Spirit. The nightstands on either side of the bed hold Tiffany-style lamps that remind me of special times in Europe where I spent part of my childhood in the early '70s; it was a place where Hemingway still seemed present, amid the cafés and ramshackle bookshops. On one nightstand are two small, hardcover books that have sat next to my bed for thirty-six years since I got sober. They are my lucky charms! One is the *Twenty-Four Hour a Day* book I got in treatment; the other is the *A Day at a Time* book given to me by my counselor, Winnie S., who the first day of group, focused her eyes like a laser on me and then with a touch of nastiness, said, "What are you doing back here?" That was my second rehab. With all the force of her twenty-five years of sobriety, she confronted the crap out of me for an hour!

I went to her office after group and still in "super-alcoholic-control-mode," said, "I don't think it's going to work out with you and me. Could you transfer me to my old counselor?"

Her quick response was, "You mean the counselor where you went out and used again?" She seemed to enjoy nailing me with that! I had no answer. Then with kindness she added, "If you still feel the same way in two days, I'll transfer you." Well, after twenty-eight days I loved that woman, her toughness is why I am sober all of these years later.

Even though it's been a number of years since Shyheart's death, I still sleep on my side of the king-size bed, leaving her side open. It took me two years to remove her pillows. I just couldn't bring myself to do it. I feel Shyheart there sometimes, always when I need her most. This night, I am reviewing a Carlos Castaneda book called *Wheels of Time* to prepare for a workshop I am going to give on shamanism and the code of the warrior. With each reading, I *hear* something deeper. Castaneda was the one who jump-started me into the world of shamanism; I resonated deeply with his emphasis around the impeccability of being a spiritual warrior.

Before long, I can't keep my eyes open and fall asleep. The next thing I remember is I am dreaming and I hear a little girl screaming in the distance. Inside the dream, I walk closer to the sound and realize it's my daughter Angel-Girl screaming. I start to run, searching for her; it feels like I am in a house. No matter where I look, I can't find her; I only hear her yells. This terrifies me so much I force my eyes open to wake myself up. I see my bedroom and know I am awake but immediately I realize it's not just a dream – Angel-Girl *is* screaming in her room down the hall. This is not the first time; she has bad nightmares sometimes. I jump out of bed, run for the door, trip over a corner of the bed and take a hard tumble. "Shit!" I yell. I get up, realizing I need to be careful and slow down. I walk through my bedroom door, which I always keep cracked open so I can hear her, and hurry quickly down the long hallway towards her room. There, I find her sitting up in bed surrounded by different-colored pillows with a big smile on her face, holding Cody, the tough caramel-colored bunny – a protector – and one she keeps close to her when she is scared.

"Sweetie, are you okay? I heard you yelling."

"Yes, Daddy, I am okay now. Angel Kristian came and protected me!"

"What happened?" I ask, trying to bring down the panic in my voice and catch my breath.

"The monsters were in my dreams again," she reports as if it's not a big deal.

"Oh no, that must have been very scary." I sit down on the bed with her.

She nods. "But it's okay now. Angel Kristian is here with me; he is very tough and a great monster fighter."

"I never heard you talk about him."

"Well, he is a new angel I made friends with," she says. Then, she adds, "He's eleven."

"A boy angel?"

"Yup! Cool, huh?"

"I didn't know angels could be kids," I respond.

"Oh, yes," she says very seriously. "There are many angels that are kids."

"That's interesting. Is he here with us right now?" I let my clairvoyant radar go out and see if I can feel a presence in the room.

"Yup, he said he'd hang out for a little while in case the monsters don't get the message." She looks at the foot of her bed and listens. "He says we should make a special monster-spray." I figure Angel Kristian must be in her line of sight; I can sense his presence but it's not totally concrete. Sometimes angels will only appear to certain people.

"A monster-spray? Very cool! How do we make it?" I ask her.

She listens again, then replies, "Kristian says, put ten drops of lavender in the blue bottle of water that has the spray thingy and leave it out in the sun for eight hours."

"I heard blue bottles were energizers."

"Can we make it, Daddy?"

"Absolutely. Does Kristian say how we should use it?"

"Two ways. First, we spray my room before I go sleepy, especially around my bed and my big pillows. And then if the monsters come, spray them a lot!" She mimes spraying them with a ferocious face.

"Okay! Then that's our plan." I hesitate a moment before asking, "Angel-Girl, can you tell me what the monsters look like?"

She mimics a horrible face and says with her arms stretched over her head, "Big icky."

I reproduce her gesture with my hands over my head and ask, "Big, huh?"

She nods rapidly in agreement.

"Hmm." I hesitate a moment, listening inside, wondering if it's too soon to share what I know with her. But very quickly I get that familiar "go" signal in my Spirit. "You know, the Holy Men used to tell me that the more powerful a warrior you are, the bigger the monsters are."

She gets a puzzled look on her face and says, "But I'm just a little girl."

"Yes, I know, but you are my daughter, born on the day the wind moved through the aspens."

She appears super-confused now and says, "I don't understand. That's the day you were born, Daddy. Like the Holy Men told you, the day the wind went –" (she makes a "whoosh-sound") "through the Cozy-White-Tree-People." That's her special name for aspens! She loves hugging them.

I interlace my fingers and bring them in front of my chest.

She stares intensely at my hands, moving into the "seeing" place. Then she suddenly gets what I have been trying to communicate, "Wow, you mean the same thing happened the day I was born and the day you were born?"

"A Ho, my Angel-Girl." I respond, using the sacred acknowledgment of a pure truth.

"What does it mean?" she asks with a concerned voice.

I put my head down, letting my Spirit go very quiet to listen inside. I know she understands what I am doing and will sit quietly with me unless…

She says suddenly, "Do you see monsters too?" She seems awed by the possibility.

I nod with certainty. For years, when I was kid and even as an adult, I had nightmares. They were terrible and left me rattled when I woke up. They were very hard to describe, like something ominous pressing in on me. Not that long ago, I made a decision to embrace those terrifying feelings when they showed up in a dream. Instead of trying to get away from them, I went towards the terror. Then deeper into it. After that, I never had those nightmares again.

"So 'cause I'm your daughter our monsters are very big?"

"That's right. Can you ask Angel Kristian if the monsters hate or like the monster-spray?"

She looks hard at me, not really understanding my question but trusting I have a reason for asking it. "Okay," she says. I see her whisper to the foot of the bed where I can begin to really feel Kristian's presence.

She looks surprised as she listens deeply to Kristian, "Really?" Then, she turns to me, "Daddy, Angel Kristian says the monsters like the spray!"

I nod confirming what I suspected.

"I don't understand," she blurts out, just short of a pout.

"Warriors make friends with the monsters."

Her eyes go big. "Really?"

"Yup."

"But they are very icky!"

"Maybe they think we are icky," I counter.

"Why? I didn't do anything to them!"

I chuckle, "I know, baby." That quiets her. "My daughter, warriors like you and me, hug the monsters. We hug scary and make friends with it."

"'Cause it makes us strong?" she asks.

I look at her very seriously and say proudly, "A Ho, Angel-Girl."

She hesitates a moment, absorbing all this, and then with a big smile she says, "I am a good hugger."

"You definitely are!" I open my arms and she jumps into them, hugging me tight.

"I am excited to see the monsters again!" she announces.

I glance over to the foot of the bed where I felt Angel Kristian's presence and very slowly I see a little boy with brown hair and brown eyes come into focus. I look closer and I can see his white wings. He smiles at me with a smile that is pure love. Then, he interlaces his little fingers together, holding them in front of his chest, showing me he is with "us." I bow my head slowly, hoping he knows how deeply grateful I am. He returns my bow and holds one hand up to say goodbye, a light shining brightly from his eyes, and then he quickly disappears. I hug my Angel-Girl closer, feeling the wind rush through the Cozy-White-Tree-People.

Chapter Sixteen

The Choice
(Angel-Girl at nine years old)

It's Saturday night and as I'm tucking my daughter in she asks, "Dad, tell me another story about you and my uncles!" She refers to the Holy Men as her uncles; she has become very close to them over the years. We visit them in the Northern Plains annually, sometimes twice a year, and she stays attached to them during our trips. They see her gifts and I just step back and let them teach her.

"Again? I'm running out of stories!"

"In the beginning when you first met them, that's my favorite part." She implores me in that *deeply wanting* tone only a nine year old can have – one that you can't say no to! Each moment is so new to them.

"Oh, you mean when they were beating up on your poor old dad!"

"Exactly!"

We laugh. "Okay." I pull my special, big green armchair over to her bed.

"Not yet!" she yells. "I have to bring over the bears that haven't heard the stories!"

"Of course," I tell her. She gets out of bed and collects two of her stuffed bears and two stuffed rabbits from different locations and sets them up on pillows so they are facing me and tucks her blanket around them and herself. She holds Bear-That-Waves facing out so he can hear too.

"We're ready!" The excitement is bursting out of her.

"You sure?"

"Definitely!"

"Hmm, what one haven't I told you, guys?" I have let the many stories about my experiences over twenty-five years with the Holy Men flow out based on the dictates of Spirit. I feel strongly that each story is a teaching tool for Angel. So I let myself go quiet for a moment, close my eyes, and see what flows up. Angel-Girl knows what I am doing. I think she likes it because it adds a feeling of magic and mystery for her. Quickly coming to mind is a special day over twenty years ago in the high mountains and just the remembrance of that powerful moment makes me say out loud, "Wow." I nod my head up and down confirming to myself that this is the *one*. "Okay, I got it!"

Angel-Girl's blue eyes are totally focused on me, not wanting to miss one word. All the bears and rabbits are in deep listening too.

"Well, you know in the beginning your uncles were very tough on me."

She nods her head up and down quickly – meaning let's get on with it!

"One really beautiful spring day, Black Hawk and I were out hiking in the mountains; we were way up – really high on this rock plateau, like the ones you and I have walked on. I had been learning from them for about two years and had spent a lot of time hiking, traveling, and just hanging out with them. You know how much that meant to me. Your dad really changed."

"Like how?" she asks curiously but with an undercurrent of confusion, as if she is thinking: *Dad is always the same – he doesn't change.*

"Well, I felt a deep connection to the Mother Earth and I felt my heart more. You could say I felt *simpler* – meaning I was quieter inside. Make sense?"

She nods, the concern on her face relaxing, relieved that the dad-change wasn't something heavy.

"So Black Hawk and I were moving over this flat plateau of bare rock; he was about thirty feet in front of me and I saw him break into a little run, then leap over a gap in the rock, landing easily on the other side. When I got to the same spot I stopped. The gap was a forty-foot drop! If you fell you would be killed – period."

"What did you do, Dad?" Angel-Girl says in hushed tone like she's afraid her voice will make me fall into the hole.

"Well, the leap felt a little too far. Your uncle stopped and waited on the other side. I didn't say anything. I just checked the distance from one side to the other. Then I studied the space to the left and to the right and the gap only widened – there was no place that was narrow or safer. I tried to imagine myself running and taking off on the spot he launched from and leaping to the other side and it just felt three feet too far."

"Wow! What happened?"

"I paced back and forth for a long time, trying to figure it out. Black Hawk stood on the other side, just watching – he didn't say anything. What I remember was how he watched me. It felt…" I think for a moment, trying to find a word she would understand. "…patient."

"Like you are with me."

"Really? You never told me that."

"I didn't want to give you a big head!"

"What!"

She giggles and hides under the covers with Bear-That-Waves.

"Oh yes, you're a good teacher."

"Wow, thanks, baby."

She comes out of hiding and says, "Keeping going!" as her head bobs up her dark hair hair flops over her face. She peeks out between the strands, looking like a wild-child. Her mother would dig it.

"Your uncle was just quietly watching me. He was only fifteen feet away. Finally, I called over to him, 'I don't think I can make it. It's just a little too far. Is there another way we can go?'

"He took a long moment and then said confidently, 'Greg, I think you can make it.'"

"They believe in you, Dad," Angel-Girl says with confidence.

"Thanks, baby." It always makes me feel good when I see that my daughter gets me. "So I just nodded at him and doubled my focus to figure out how to do this. I walked back to where I would start, then made a slow practice run and hit my right foot on the exact spot I would push off from and lifted my leg as if I was going to leap. *Okay, I got it*, I thought. *I can do this.* I returned to the starting point, setting myself in position, getting ready to go as I looked at the place I would land. And then that forty-foot drop loomed up in my mind and I froze. I got really scared. I could feel the fear rushing though me, causing my legs to shake."

"You were scared? Really?" she asks shocked, as if I could never be afraid.

"Yeah, I was. I just didn't feel like I could do it." Even though I was in pretty good shape and spent a lot of time in the mountains, I had never made a leap like this without being roped. "So I looked over at your uncle, still sensing only patience from him. I decided to back down and just breathe for a moment."

"Like you taught me!" she blurts out, as if she's just found the right answer on a test.

"You got it! I went back and studied the gap, I guess hoping to see something that would make me feel safer – nothing. *Come on, Greg*, I said to myself. I was getting angry and went back to the starting place I marked. I just stood there, frozen. I could not make myself go. I had this vision that kept coming into my head of just missing the edge and slipping and falling to my death. It seemed really possible that could happen."

"You could have died?" I can feel the fear in her voice.

"It was possible, baby. But don't forget this was like twenty years before you were born. If this is scaring you, I can tell another story."

She jumps up on the bed. "NO! Tell me what happened!'

I laugh. "Okay! Get cozy again." As she gets back under the covers with the bears and rabbits, she pulls the blanket up to her chin so that she and Bear-That-Waves are in semi-hiding.

"I felt totally paralyzed," I continue. "The fear felt enormous! I didn't remember ever feeling that way before. Finally, I just made a decision to give up. I couldn't do it. I looked across at Black Hawk and shook my head, not having any words to say to him. I was so disappointed in myself."

My daughter is listening harder than she ever has before, with the exception of those times when we talk about her mother. She seems stunned into silence – the father she knows doesn't give up.

"Your uncle sat down cross-legged on the rock surface, facing me, and said these words, which I will never forget: 'Greg, I know in my heart you can do it. If you don't try, this will be the last time we will walk the path of power together.'"

"What did he mean, Dad?" Angel-Girl seems almost scared to ask me this, as if she knows the answer.

"He meant he would no longer teach me or hang out with me."

"Really?"

"Yup, you know Black Hawk, he meant it."

"Why would he say that? You are his brother."

"Well, this was before your father became a true brother to your uncles – this happened way in the beginning, before that."

She looks at me not knowing whether to be confused or angry. She decides on anger.

"That was icky," she says with a big pout and I'm not sure how to respond to that; it never occurred to me she would look at it like that but it makes perfect sense from a daughter's perspective.

"I can understand why you would feel like that. But your uncles are very smart, right?"

She nods reluctantly, still frowning.

"I was shocked too when I heard him say that. But I also knew why he said it, baby. He was willing to give up our friendship to force me to find the courage to believe in myself. I thought that was pretty awesome and I admired him for it. Does that make any sense?"

"Sort of."

"Should I keep going?"

"I guess," she says not very enthusiastically.

"You sure?"

She nods, and I can tell she doesn't know what to think of her uncle.

"Okay. So I just stared at him in disbelief, trying to reject in my mind what he just said; a chill went through me. I had spent enough time with him to know he was very serious and to respond in some way was fruitless and also disrespectful. I was even more scared now. To lose his friendship, his mentoring was unthinkable. But it could mean my death. This was not a movie out here in the mountains, this was real life. I gazed across the space at him, seeing the dark fierceness in his face that I had come to know since the day I met him – it was the face of a warrior. You have seen that face on your uncles, right?"

"On your face too, Dad," she says, like she's trying to take care of me.

I smile humbly in acknowledgment.

"I felt the wind start to come up a little. I stood looking at him for a long time. I was speechless. He never took his eyes off me. I decided to sit down and try to settle myself. I knew this moment was a teaching. We sat across from one another, him on one side, me on the other, the blue sky surrounding us; the wind, our friend, beginning to swirl around us. After a moment, he closed his eyes and started to sing. It was a song I had heard many times and it always touched a deep, hidden part of me, as if taking me back to another lifetime. His voice filled the big space around us. I closed my eyes, feeling his chanting wash over me, quieting my mind. The wind grew stronger.

Suddenly, I heard the faint sound of drumming behind me."

Angel-Girl's eyes go big. "Who was there?"

"I turned around to see but there was nothing but wide open space. It got stronger! Boom, boom, boom! It was so real; unlike the special 'hearing' we do."

"Wow!"

"I turned back and your uncle's singing got louder and then I heard something that I can still hear to this day, twenty-five years later: a group of men's voices singing behind me, matching Black Hawk's words!"

"It was the Old Ones, wasn't it?" she asks, awed.

"That's right, baby, it was. Even though I had felt their presence many times, it was never as *real* as this. I knew not to turn around. Their singing went deep into my soul."

"They were honoring you, Dad," she says proudly.

"A Ho," I confirm. "I felt a physical power growing in me. I opened my eyes and your uncle was peering directly at me, his dark eyes opened wide, shining power at me – his Black Hawk was in his eyes!"

"Cool!" When animal totems show up in stories Angel-Girl's excitement always rises.

"Suddenly, a phrase that I learned from your uncles came to me. I thought I understood its meaning but now I *felt* its meaning: 'Hoka-hey,' which sort of means, 'Today is a good day to die.'"

She squints her blue eyes at me, suddenly pulled from

her super-focus, not understanding. "What does that mean, Dad?" she asks me, concerned.

"It's a little hard to explain…" I ponder for a moment a way to describe its meaning to her. "Think of it this way: If Bear-That-Waves was in trouble and it meant you might get really hurt saving him, what would you do?"

Then she says something so powerful, so surprising, that I realize my nine-year-old daughter is way beyond her years and beyond most adults, "There is no choice, my father."

I peer deeply into her eyes, which are steady, focused – I feel her mother looking back at me. I nod my head firmly for there are no words.

"That is Hoka-hey, Angel-Girl. The willingness to risk everything and to do it with joy and acceptance. But also, it could mean, 'Let's Go!' "So I whispered 'Hoka-hey' to myself to see how it felt. The sound of the words coming from my mouth seemed very familiar to me."

"Hoka-hey," she whispers into Bear-That-Waves's soft, golden ear as if they are magic words.

"I felt myself get laser-focused, as if all the energy in my body was focused at the same time; I had never experienced anything like it. The power surging in me pushed me up on my feet and Black Hawk stood up on the other side and raised his arms over his head, singing to the sky. The wind was blowing hard now, the singing and drumming of the Old Ones grew stronger behind me; my body, my soul moving to its rhythm. My whole being vibrated with power and then I said those words to myself in a passionate determined voice I didn't recognize, 'Hoka-hey!'"

Angel-Girl squeezes Bear-That-Waves tighter, her whole being hanging on my every word.

"I started to run towards the edge and when I got to that spot I leapt over the gap, feeling the forty-foot drop pass below me; it was like I flew! I landed on the other side with plenty of room to spare. I stood still for a long moment facing the big sky, not quite believing I did it. Then I turned around to your uncle and raised my palm and said, 'A Ho.' I hoped he saw how deeply grateful I was. He raised his hand and made a strong nod of his head and said, 'A Ho.' Then I faced the other side and 'saw' the Old Ones standing there; six of them, dressed in native clothing."

"Awesome! There were six of them?"

"Yes! They looked very fierce. It was like they knew me! I raised my hand to them, 'A Ho, Old Ones, A Ho. My heart is full.' They raised their palms in return and then slowly faded into the air. I left a little tobacco to honor them. And as you know, my daughter, I have been walking the path of power with the Holy Men since."

"That's my favorite story! You were really brave."

"Thanks, baby. About a year went by and I was sitting with them in a diner having breakfast and it occurred to me to ask Black Hawk something. I said, 'Do you remember that day on the rock when I felt I couldn't make that leap?' Well, your uncle just nodded but I saw a twinkle in his eyes, which I had learned to take as an alert to watch out, something might be coming. I asked him, 'What would have happened if I didn't make it?' He smiled and said sort of formally, 'Do you remember, before you leapt, that at the very moment you stood up, I stood up with you?' 'Yes,' I said. There was something about the way he said, 'with you,' that felt...." I point to my chest, meaning it touched me. "He said, 'When I stood up and you started to run, I moved closer to the ledge so if you started to fall I could reach out and grab you.' I stared at him, trying to remember that day…that's right! When I landed he was standing behind me!"

"Wow, he wouldn't have let you fall! That's my uncle!"

"That's right, that is *your uncle*, a true warrior. When I realized what he had done I was so deeply grateful. Then I made this gesture, which you know…" I moved my hand, palming face down quickly in front of me with authority.

"That means, 'It is good,' right?"

"Good girl! That's right."

"The path without words, Dad."

"A Ho, my Angel. And it wasn't long after that, that I became their brother."

Chapter Seventeen

Dinosaurs
(Angel-Girl at nine years old)

It's an early Wednesday evening in October and Angel-Girl and I are on our way to her fourth-grade teacher-parent meeting. We have been quiet for most of the fifteen-minute ride. But I feel Angel-Girl scrutinizing me, trying to gauge my mood.

"Now, you promised, right?" she asks from the back seat of the Explorer. She is referring to my *supposed* edginess at these school meetings. I just have a problem with the whole education system, and sometimes I can't help myself! My grandmother and dad were teachers so I have a special place in my heart for educators. But when it comes to Angel-Girl's schooling, I have a blind spot and can get a touch direct with the teachers. I'm aware of my super-protectiveness over the *teaching* of my apprentice-in-training. I was okay when she was in kindergarten and first and second grade but since third grade, the protective energy has ratcheted up. Maybe because she is coming into her shamanic gifts so quickly and I fear them being detoured. I'm working on trying to change my attitude, but there is a missing reason for my edginess that I haven't discovered yet.

"Yes, of course. Excellent. Outstanding," I assure her.

"Daddy, you are doing your Hugh Grant imitation!"

I chuckle. She's right! We stop at the red light.

"Please don't make a fuss," she says. "You make the teachers nervous."

"No worries, baby. I will be good." I turn around quickly, giving her my best "nice guy absolutely-in-control" face. During these school meetings something comes over me and I tend to move out of deep listening with the teachers and into disagreement-listening or "are they messing with my daughter's gifts-listening?" I try to be funny about it but according to my daughter it doesn't always come off that way. Again, some part of the reason is a mystery to me. I ask her, "Haven't I gotten a lot better?"

"Sort of. But you promised, remember." I can feel the suspicion in her voice. "Mrs. Philips *is super-nice*." Meaning I don't have to chop her head off.

We pull up to the Fairfield Elementary School, get out, and walk to the front entrance, hand in hand. I see her watching my stride.

"Daddy, you are walking like your panther." I can't get away with anything with this child! "You are going to scare everyone!"

"Sorry, baby. Dad will be cool." She levels me with a serious look, meaning stop it! It's the same expression her mother, Shyheart, would use on me.

"I promise," I tell her. If you think I am protective over Angel-Girl, my panther-brother can get scary. He just flashed out of me as I was walking. In my mind, I say to him, "Easy, brother, easy. We have to learn to trust these people." I sense him ease back but see him raise the corner of his lip, baring his teeth and letting out an unhappy growl. Once in a while, I will laugh to myself at the thought of anyone trying to break into our home! God help them. My guess is my panther would project himself right out of the dreamweave and tackle the intruder.

We walk through the front doors and into the school hallway lined with half-a-dozen doors leading to classrooms. On the hallway walls are kids' drawings of their families or homes or favorite animals. I see her teacher, Mrs. Philips, is standing outside the door to the classroom. I guess she remembered my comment at the last parent group meeting where I stood up and requested, as nicely as I could, that they work on the scheduling of teacher-parent meetings. And then I threw in, "If I wanted to wait this long I'd hang out at the DMV!" Afterwards, I sheepishly thought maybe it was a little passive-aggressive. But I felt better since it did get a laugh from the other parents who nodded in agreement. Consent from your peers is a powerful justification!

Mrs. Philips appears to be in her late thirties, with dark brown hair in a bun and a Mediterranean complexion. I notice her attire of tailored slacks, heels, and a crisp button-down shirt – a little too business-like for me. I feel that edginess poke its head out of my emotional body. But then I spot a cool, three-strand bracelet of blue lapis beads on her right wrist and I feel the edginess pull back. I laugh in my head, thinking, *Could you be any more judgmental, pal?* As I move closer, I see a glint of innate humor in her eyes.

She waves. "Mr. Drambour, welcome. Good to see you."

I feel Angel-Girl squeeze my hand in warning. I nod and give Mrs. Philips a formal, "Good evening." I can hear my guard go up subtly in the tone of my voice. And I am sure my seer-daughter hears it too, given the way she tightens her grip on my hand, almost causing it to go numb! I heed her warning and take a breath, trying to quiet my thinking.

As we shake hands, Mrs. Philips smiles at my daughter, "Hi, Angel!"

"Hi, Mrs. Philips!"

"Please come in." At this school, they encourage the parents to have the child sit in. I really like that, remembering my own experiences of these meetings as a child when I would wonder, *What are these secrets my parents and teachers are talking about?* I felt left out and as if there was some agenda they were keeping from me.

Mrs. Philips escorts us into the classroom and points to the *one* other adult chair in the room other than hers. (Another request I had submitted. I guess these teachers talk to each other! They usually make the parents try to fit into one of the children's desks. No one would ever accuse of me of not being assertive!) "I am so glad you came tonight. Angel is a very special student and doing well in all her subjects. She has quite an imagination! Her math...."

I interrupt her, "Mrs. Philips, forgive me for interrupting, but I am little concerned about something."

"Oh yes, please tell me," she responds with such kindness that it disarms me and makes me rethink what I was going to ask, which now seems ridiculous but I feel committed.

"Angel told me the other day you were very focused on teaching the kids the importance of dinosaur poop. Is that true?" When I hear this query come out of my mouth, inside I'm shaking my head, thinking, *What is wrong with you, brother? You sound like a jerk!*

"I'm sorry?" Mrs. Philips looks at me, totally baffled. I feel my daughter eyeballing me from the side.

"No, Father," Angel says, "I told you that Jimmy asked Mrs. Philips if dinosaurs pooped. And she said, of course they do and told us you could see what they were eating that way." The dreaded designation of "Father" has shown up. Oh God, I am really in trouble now!

I try to cover with, 'That makes perfect sense." I feel Mrs. Philips studying me without appearing obvious about it. It doesn't feel intrusive, more of a concern. I hear all my spiritual teachers in my head, reminding me how you can perceive some wild stuff when you are out of your innate mental-health or wisdom. It's obvious to me I am just looking for something to complain about.

"So, Angel's math skills need a little more attention," Mrs. Philips continues, as if totally unfazed by my weirdness.

"Math?" I question. I feel a defensiveness in my voice that surprises me. I immediately recognize this touches some personal memory about my having trouble with not "getting" math easily – it made me feel like there was something wrong with me.

"Yes," Mrs. Phillips responds, seeming to wonder at my confusion.

"Angel, how big a hole does one dig to plant a six-foot Arizona Cyprus tree? Depth and width?" I think, *Sorry to bring you into this, Fred!* Angel-Girl loves Fred, the special tree that lives in our yard, so I'm sure she'll get this right. Of course, I know how important math is but I'm obviously going out of my mind at this point.

I can see by Angel-Girl's eyes and body language that she is using all her willpower not to freak out on me. She says through gritted teeth, "Three feet deep by four feet wide."

"Ah," I say, like an attorney concluding his case. It's a damn roller-coaster ride of reactions and emotions in this classroom! I calculate time zones quickly hoping one of my own spiritual teachers will still be up when we get home. I obviously need to be rescued from myself. I add up the offenses so far and how many days I will get the silent treatment from Angel. I count two. *Okay*, I think, *I can handle that.* Three days of the silent treatment is when I feel I have completely failed as a father.

"Well, we are *honored* to have Angel in the class," Mrs. Philips says, as if I haven't just made a fool of myself. This teacher is good; she can't be rattled! With her continued compassion, I realize that maybe I haven't given her a fair chance. She adds, "She contributes a great deal and is really upbeat. You have done an amazing job with her."

"Thank you," I say. There is something about the way she says "honored" that catches my attention.

"Do you have any questions, Mr. Drambour?"

I glance over at Angel-Girl who has now graduated to a PhD level of non-verbal communication. She's shooting death rays at me with her blue eyes, once again reflecting her mother. "Yes, I do." I smile brightly, trying to redeem myself by lightening up and injecting a little humor, "This year, will there be any tutoring on how to turn into a dinosaur?"

Mrs. Philips adjusts herself so she is straighter in her seat and as she gazes at me, I notice there's a little sparkle in her eyes. Then she says, "Well, Mr. Drambour, if I have to be honest, I was really excited to be teaching the daughter of the man considered to be the definitive teacher on shape-shifting."

I try to suppress it but can't help but grin and chuckle. I feel very proud she was aware of my work. I bow my head and say, "You are very kind."

We laugh together and it feels good. It occurs to me it

might be the first time I have laughed with a woman like this since Shyheart.

Then she says, super-friendly, "I have studied your work and I've watched a number of your videos on YouTube – they're very powerful. It's an honor to finally meet you."

I say softly, "Thank you."

"Angel, do you have any questions?" Mrs. Philips asks her.

"Yes. Which dinosaurs eat their father – slowly?" We all laugh.

"Well, that could be your homework!"

It's nice to feel a lightness in the room. I didn't realize how much I missed it.

"So, she is doing well?" I ask.

"Yes, very well. She loves to create! I am not too worried about the math. Some children just get it suddenly. The only thing I might mention is…"

I feel Angel-Girl shift in her seat. "Sometimes, during play-time she spends too much time alone. Her two best friends, Sam and Bobby, moved away. So, I am a little concerned."

I was upset myself about them moving. The *three leaves* broken up. I say, "They were very important to her."

"Angel and I have talked about this, right?" she asks Angel-Girl.

She nods, obviously not wanting to get into it. There's a sad, almost angry look on her face.

We sit quietly for a moment. When the twins, Sam and

Bobby, moved to another state during the summer. I just kept acknowledging her feelings, very committed to not trying to fix her. This was a struggle of mine when she was younger. Sam and Bobby accepted her and understood her and the things she did, unlike the other kids who think she is weird because she likes talking to the Tree-People. One could say they buffeted her and now that they are not here, she's back to not understanding why other kids don't get her.

Mrs. Philips asks her with a firm, but gentle tone, "Angel, you are a shaman's daughter, yes?"

She nods at Mrs. Philips, the tears starting to well up in her eyes.

"You see the world much differently than the other children. Maybe even much differently than most adults!" Then, she says excitedly, "This is your gift! What a gift to have! You are so very lucky."

I see Angel-Girl start to listen deeply. Even though these are things I have told her a million times, I see how important it is for her to hear this from someone else. My own teaching about honoring partnerships flashes in my mind. I need to honor this partnership with teachers more and stop coming from a place of disagreement or fear.

Mrs. Philips adds, "You just be yourself and another best friend will show up. It has too! But you have to try and not close up. Okay?"

"Okay," Angel-Girl responds, seeming to feel better, more hopeful.

"Good," says Mrs. Philips, grinning at Angel's change in mood. The meeting comes to an end and she escorts us into the hallway and we say goodbye, I am trying not to grimace from the nail that Angel-Girl is digging into my palm. I guess even though she feels better, she has not forgiven me for coming on too strong!

As we walk down the hall, Mrs. Philips calls after me, "Mr. Drambour." I turn around to find her looking at me with a serious focus but at the same appearing a little nervous. Her posture is subtly more erect. She raises her left palm slowly, apprehensively, as if to ask, *Is my gesture okay?* This is the honoring gesture I use when I sign off at the end of my videos. The presence of Spirit fills the hallway. I feel her connecting with me, seeing me. I turn purposely so I am facing her completely and raise my palm, returning the gesture. I'm a little blown-away by the moment. A deep sense of humility comes into my heart and I mouth silently, "Thank you," hoping she understands this means I am really grateful to her for putting up with my nonsense and helping my daughter.

She gently nods and with a gracious smile, says, "Take care!"

Wow, I think, *This is a very special woman.*

Angel grabs my hand and we walk out to the car. When we get outside the building she abruptly drops my hand and stomps over to the back car-door and stands waiting with her arms folded across her chest!

Oh no, I think. I unlock the car with the remote and she

opens her door quickly and jumps in and fastens her seat belt, before I have a chance to do it. Something she knows I love doing. She stares straight ahead, with her angry face. I'm not sure how much of it is real anger or how much is "I should be angry but I'm really not." I jump into the driver's seat and try to catch a glimpse of her in the rearview mirror. She just stares straight ahead – purposely not acknowledging me. This is how she tortures me.

I pull out of the parking lot and make a right and head down the short street to 89A, our main thoroughfare. There's light traffic tonight. I give Angel-Girl a few minutes and then I say, "That Mrs. Philips is a very special teacher."

"I told you!" Big attitude. But I have learned to ignore it – most of the time!

"I thought I did a little better tonight. At least, it ended pretty well!" I say, trying to be upbeat.

I can see her in the mirror, giving me the "are you kidding?" look.

"Sorry, baby." I say, trying to tell her I was just being Dad. No response.

After a minute, she says, "I'm glad you like her, Daddy. I thought you would."

"You were right."

"Her husband went to heaven."

"Really?"

I look in the rearview mirror and see her nod with sad eyes.

"How come you didn't tell me before?"

"I didn't want you to be sad."

I get it now, that's what the feeling of connection was about. Mrs. Philips knows we lost Shyheart. Wow! I feel really grateful she saw me.

Then something suddenly dawns on me and it's so big I pull the Explorer over to the curb and sit in silence for a moment.

"What's wrong, Daddy?"

I turn around to face her, "I just got something. I finally understand why I am a big grizzly bear in these meetings. Your mother planned on home-schooling you, which I wanted too. And if she was here that's what would have happened. She was super-excited about it; it was important to her. She was home-schooled you know until high school. So…" I stop myself, feeling a rush of feelings.

"I understand, Daddy." She looks at me with such deep understanding it helps me forgive myself for being so weird. Then she says, "Mommy is always in school with me, watching me! And you teach me a lot of important stuff." Going all formal, she adds, "Father!"

I laugh and we continue down the road, turning into our neighborhood. It occurs to me how one person's kindness, in this case Mrs. Philips's, can spark an insight. I thank her one more time in my heart.

Then, I hear Angel's voice from the back, "Dad?"

"Yeah, baby?"

"You know, I already know how to turn into a dinosaur."

I chuckle, "I know you do."

"When we get home can I use the computer before I go to bed?"

"Sure. Homework?"

She nods at me in the rearview mirror with a little devilish smile, "Google search for father-eating-dinosaurs!"

Chapter Eighteen

Little Warrior Tree
(Angel-Girl at ten and a half years old)

As we're driving back from Flagstaff on 89A, Angel-Girl asks me, "Dad, can we stop and say hello to your sister, the Little Warrior Tree?" I pick up an inflection of concern in her voice – not sure what it's about.

"Sure, honey." There is something about the Warrior Tree that always pulls at her. "It's coming up here in a little bit. Keep your eye out for it."

A half-mile later…

"There's the place to park!" she yells so loud it makes me jump. Even at ten and a half, she has not lost one bit of her child-like excitement for adventure.

"Okay!" I yell back, laughing. I pull onto the wide shoulder, park, and we get out and walk up the side of the road, holding hands. A few cars whiz by. She is on my right, buzzing with energy. Fifty yards up the road we arrive at a big tree-break, which is a gap between the trees about seventy-five feet wide. This is the entrance for the route to the Little Warrior Tree. It's a giant, boulder-debris field that goes straight up through the forest for three-quarters of a mile. The pitch is about 35 degrees – a very steep and dangerous climb, especially coming down. You could get into serious trouble here – and I mean serious – life-threatening. At the top is a lava-boulder field, five acres in size and 6000-feet in elevation. In this field of lava boulders, there is only one little six-foot juniper tree growing out of the crack in an enormous sharp-edged boulder. This is the Little Warrior Tree! It's a very tough tree to be able to thrive in this exposed place with the big storms and wind. She is my sister in the shamanic tradition, a hard-core survivor. She is a big part of my Sedona story.

We stand gazing up at the corridor of debris. It always looks ominous, mysterious, menacing. Over the years this climb has gotten more difficult to navigate because the brush keeps growing denser and thicker. I usually go in winter when the leaves have dropped off, which makes going up the boulder field easier.

"This is the first place you found, right, Dad?" my daughter asks me, always deeply curious about the origins of my work. The perfect apprentice!

"Yup, this is the one," I answer quietly, reverently. This is the first place of power I found here in Sedona many years before Angel-Girl was born. I was moving off-trail through the trees on the other side of the road and felt a strong physical pull over to where we are standing and then felt drawn straight up and discovered the Little Warrior Tree! I sensed real power and energy emanating there, much like I experienced back in the Northern Plains with the Holy Men. Even though I didn't feel like I could guide clients up to that location because of the dangers, it made me believe I could work here. It opened the door and I found more places of power or sacred areas to which I now guide clients. Periodically, I will visit the Little Warrior Tree and hang out with her, to listen and talk about our lives.

"The Little Warrior Tree is up there all alone?" Angel-Girl asks me, a tangible worry in her voice.

"You could say she is, baby. But she has lots of very big Rock-People to keep her company," I assure her. She is very sensitive to anything being alone. While I've always felt this has to do with losing her mom at such a young age, I've sensed there is also something more to it. I have tried to discover what that is over the years but she just shuts down if I try to probe more deeply.

She stares hard up at the hill. If I didn't know better, I'd say she was doing what I used to do when I was younger, more agile, and braver – plotting the best route to take to make this dangerous climb.

"Honey, are you okay?"

She turns to me with an intense, purposeful glance that surprises me. I've seen this expression before but never on her. Her eyes are like those of the Holy Men – the eyes of a warrior. Then, she solemnly and slowly pats her chest twice, then looks back up at the boulder field.

I understand right away what she is communicating.

"You are feeling the Little Warrior Tree?" I ask her, softly.

She nods adamantly then circles the index finger and thumb of both hands together and interlocks them in front of her face and pushes them forward. This is our sign for together in spirit. The path without words. She suddenly seems far older than ten and a half.

"When do I get to go visit her?" she asks, a deliberate tone in her question. She's been pleading to go for a few years but I don't feel she is big enough yet for the climb.

I study her height and then position my hand a foot over her head, "When you get to be about this height, I will take you! I think probably a year – no more."

"Dad, I'm big enough and I'm a good climber. Can't we go right now? I have my hiking shoes on and we have water and I have my special bracelet on." She raises her wrist to show me. The bracelet is strung with gold luminescent glass beads, each one the color of a mountain lion's eyes. It was a gift from the Holy Men to honor the meeting of her totem. She has not taken it off in two years. To say it's precious to her would be an understatement!

"You are a good climber," I reply. "There's no doubt about that. But this is very dangerous and much different than anything we have ever done. You can get seriously hurt in this place. You are going to have to trust your old man." Just the thought of taking her up here scares the hell out of me. It's called a debris field for a reason, it's like the aftermath of a tornado. There are meshes of vines waiting to tangle around your feet; six-foot branches sticking up like spears; unstable rocks that collapse when you put your weight on them; giant slick boulders where you can't get a grip; cobwebs all over the place; and let's not even go into what might be crawling around. It's like climbing through a mine field. One small slip or fall and she could be injured – or worse.

She narrows her eyes at me, not too happy, then peers back up at the boulders. I hear the tiniest of growls come from her and "see" her mountain lion totem is starting to superimpose over her. I chuckle.

"Angel-Girl, shape-shifting here is not going to change my mind!"

"She's a good climber! The little tree is lonely up there!" she implores, the wanting in her voice is hard to say no to, but I have to.

"Of course she loves to climb. That's what mountain lions do! But if I let you climb this now, your warrior mother would reach down from heaven and kill me!"

More barely audible growls.

"You want to say the prayer?" I ask her, hoping this will deflect her.

"Really?" She knows invoking the prayer is an honor.

"Absolutely. The little tree would love it."

"How do I start?"

"Like we usually do, just trust your words. It will come." I hand her a pinch of tobacco to offer. She holds it against her heart.

"Okay." She takes a long moment, slowing her breathing down. I place my palms on my chest and bow my head, closing my eyes.

She begins. She is always passionate and deeply sincere when she prays but I hear an added intensity today: "A Ho, Old Ones. It is Angel-Girl, blood sister to the mountain lion, daughter to Bear-That-Walks-Softly and Shyheart. I greet you, my heart is full. I send many blessings to all the Grandfather and Grandmother Rock-and Tree-People in this sacred place. Thank you for honoring us. I send many blessings to the Little Warrior Tree, sister to my father, and I hope someday to be your sister too. You have honored our family and helped my father – thank you, thank you. Soon, I will get to hug you, me and my lion sister." I can hear emotion rushing up in her voice with these last words about hugging the tree, causing her to hesitate, and then she says, "I am Angel-Girl…" Her voice breaks, shaking with feeling, then she repeats it again fervently as if reminding herself who she is, "I am Angel-Girl!"

Suddenly, I sense her running! I open my eyes and she has bolted up the boulder field! I yell at her, "Angel! What are you doing?" *Oh my God!* I think.

"Baby, STOP!" She starts to scramble up the first set of boulders. "STOP! THAT'S AN ORDER!" She gets quickly to the first plateau 100 feet away and stands on top of a big grey boulder, turns, faces me, raises her little arms above her head, and screams through her tears with a voice filled with unbelievable fierceness:

"I AM ANGEL-GIRL, BLOOD SISTER TO THE MOUNTAIN LION, I AM ANGEL-GIRL! HOKA-HEY, MY FATHER! HOKA-HEY!"

Hoka-hey? What? *Today is a good day to die!* I am in such shock I'm frozen. She quickly turns and starts to scramble up.

I have no choice but to leap over and start to climb after her…I can see the debris corridor has worsened since my last climb: more twenty- to forty-foot trees have fallen, crisscrossing the corridor, teetering precariously; it's a bad accident waiting to happen. Every fiber of my being is firing with fear at the possibility of her falling – all it would take is one slip and she could slam her head into rock. I breathe, trying to center myself and not panic.

She continues to scurry up, maybe 150 feet in front of me. Even though she is half my size, she is quicker than me and her innocence of the dangers here helps her. I realize there is only one way I might catch her and that is to shape-shift into my panther. But then it occurs to me that if she notices I'm gaining on her, she might rush and make a fatal mistake. I quickly decide to hold off until she arrives at the safer section just up ahead of her and then I will turn on the speed with my panther's sure feet.

She glances back to check how far away I am. She's focused, no fear on her face. I know at this point threats of *you are going to be grounded for life* are fruitless. There was something about her invocation that told me she is on a mission and I am caught between admiring her and being angry.

So I go with being logical and yell up to her: "Angel-Girl, do you know how to find the Little Warrior Tree?"

No response, just more scrambling. I stop for a moment to catch my breath and watch her. She is moving extremely well, cautiously and deftly, around obvious danger spots. *Not too bad*, I think. *She has really learned how to move in tricky terrain.* I feel an urge to shout up my pride but then I think that would condone this total disobedience. The other problem here is if I catch her, then what? I can't pick her up and carry her back – that would be totally unsafe. The descent is where the risks get much greater, one step on a rock that collapses under you and you are hurtled forward into a sharp branch or razor-like rock. I take some comfort in knowing that no matter what, she will have to descend with me. All this is moving through my mind as we climb. I actually consider bringing her mother into it as my last trump card. I could let her know how disappointed in her – or angry – her mother would be, but that feels wrong as soon as I think it.

As we climb, the towering fir trees on both of the corridors get tighter, blocking out the sun, darkening the area.

Screw it! I think. *It's crazy but I am going counterintuitive. What's the first rule in communicating? Develop rapport.* I call up to her, "Angel-Girl, you are climbing well."

After a few yards, she stops and peers down at me. I can see her face squinting at me, trying to read me. She shouts, "Don't try any of your Jedi mind-tricks on me!"

I gaze up at her and try not to laugh. "No, I am serious, you are doing very well. Is your sister lion helping you?"

"Sort of," she says reluctantly, not really wanting to open up to me. Her thick wavy hair is all over the place with little twigs stuck in it and her face is streaked with dirt; she looks like a beautiful child that was raised by wolves.

"That's how it is sometimes when you shape-shift. Hard to explain, right?" Even though we are a hundred feet apart, our voices carry easily in the silent woods.

She nods, still studying me, trying to gauge what I am feeling. "I'm in a lot of trouble, right?" she asks but with no real fear, just wanting to know the score.

I hesitate for a moment and then something occurs to me: "Well, about as much trouble as I got in when I ran off on my own in Paris for four hours when I was ten years old!"

"Paris in France?

"That's the place!"

"Cool!"

I chuckle, "Your grandmother and great grandmother didn't think so!"

"What happened?" I sense her curiosity, despite her single-minded quest. Maybe she's hoping I'll let her off the hook.

"I came back to the hotel where we were staying and they told me they were very worried. But what I remember is them accepting it; they could see it made sense I would do that. I liked wandering around and exploring and never thought there was anything scary about it."

"I like this place a lot but it's…"

"What, baby?"

"It's sort of scary, spooky." I can hear her trying to cover her own fear.

"Yes, it is."

She stays quiet.

"You can always turn around and come down," I suggest gently.

"No! The Little Warrior Tree is lonely up there. I don't like it when things are alone."

"I know you don't. Can you ask the Little Warrior Tree if she is lonely?"

"What do you mean?" she asks suspiciously.

"Well, just 'see' the Little Warrior Tree in your mind and ask her; you know how to do that. She is not that far away."

My daughter focuses on my face, searching for a hint of trickery. I discern her wanting to believe me but then the Angel-Girl determination flashes back in her face and she pivots and starts to scamper back up the debris field. She ducks carefully under some fallen trees. So much for the idea of "seeing." I follow her. She is moving into an easier section and I estimate if I bring my panther forth I might be able to catch her. That intuitive feeling I know very well, of *wait, hold,* flows up in me again. The section just above her is the hardest part, with a steep pitch where she'll have to pull herself up over boulders the size of a small car using only her bare hands. I question if she can she do it. Kids are pretty amazing, and their lack of fear gives them the ability to do unbelievable things.

I shout to her, "That section up ahead is very tricky. Be careful!"

She just keeps going.

I watch her closely in this section, but at the same time I try to stay focused on my own movement. I see her find a foothold on the face of a large grey boulder and then another further up. As she reaches up with both hands to grab the top edge to pull herself up and over, she suddenly slips back, one hand losing her grip. "DADDY!" she screams. "I'M FALLING!" She clings to the top of the boulder with one hand, as one foot keeps slipping while the other foot appears secure in a crack. She is about 100 feet from me.

"HANG ON, BABY! I'M COMING!" I yell to her, trying to keep my voice super-confident.

I call quickly to my panther, "Come forth, my brother, come forth. We are one, the same breath."

I feel my black panther instantly come into me and I am peering out of his green eyes. I sense his big paws on the rock underneath. We focus in on my daughter and begin to accelerate, past my usual capacity and agility, leaping with total confidence from one boulder to the next. No fear of falling. I am my panther now.

"DADDY!" she screams louder. "I CAN'T HANG

ON!" I see her trying to grab the ledge with her free hand but she can't make it.

"HANG ON! YOU CAN DO IT! I'M ALMOST THERE." She is about fifty feet away now. And then I hear her say in a shocked voice, "Mommy?"

I see her pull herself up over the rock and disappear.

I scurry up over the boulder where I lost sight of her, and discover her sitting cross-legged on the rock, looking both amazed and stunned at the same time.

I feel my panther pull back inside me.

"Are you okay?" I ask, trying my best not to freak out.

"Mommy helped me." Her eyes look dazed.

"What do you mean?" I say, confused.

"I felt a hand grab my hand and I looked up and it was Mommy!" she says, not quite believing it just happened. "She pulled me up and then she was gone. She smiled at me!"

I sit down cross-legged opposite her, trying to absorb what she's saying. I'm speechless. I scan the area with my clairvoyance trying to see or feel Shyheart – nothing.

"My mommy's eyes are very blue," she tells me matter-of-factly, just wanting to report this to me. I am having a hard time speaking. I just stare at her. "Her hand was very soft, Daddy." And then, "She had your special ring on her finger." She is referring to the gold, family-insignia ring that I always wear. Shyheart and I didn't wear wedding rings; we wore matching family rings. They were *every thing* to us. Mine belonged to my older brother who passed very young and I made a duplicate for her.

"This ring, baby?" I ask holding up my ring, just to make sure.

She nods. The overwhelming tension of the climb, the terror of something terrible happening to Angel-Girl, and Shyheart's presence all crash down on me at once and I can't hold it in anymore. I put my face in my hands and start to cry in relief. She crawls over to me and puts her arms around my neck. "Daddy, I'm so sorry I disobeyed you."

"She saved you," I say. I can't stop the tears. It's just too much. My Shyheart reached over from the other side and saved our daughter. Sometimes, the magic in my life is too overwhelming. Like why do I deserve all these blessings? Even though my purpose as a shamanic healer is to look through the veil between this world and the alternative universe, this report of Shyheart pulling her up is an anomaly even for me. But I have read about such happenings and believe in them.

"Don't cry, Daddy," she beseeches me, squeezing me tighter.

"I am just happy, my Angel." I tell her, trying to calm myself down. "Just kind of blown away." I take a big breath, centering myself. "I was really scared you would get hurt here. It's so dangerous."

"I'm sorry, Daddy," she cries.

"Now, don't you start crying!" I try to joke with her. I pull her from me and guide her body so she is sitting right in front of me.

I peer deep into her eyes and see a maturity in them I haven't let myself fully acknowledge before. Sometimes, I get caught up in parenting her like I think ten year olds should be parented, instead of just trying to parent *Angel-Girl*. I think, *Man, she has grown up so fast.* We sit there for a long moment, looking gently at each other, as a deep silence permeates the dark woods around us. The path without words, brothers and sisters.

"Your uncles would be deeply proud of what you did today," I say to her, emotion resonating through my voice. I know that their pride in her is the most powerful thing I could say to her.

Her eyes go big in surprise. "Really?"

"You followed your heart and were willing to get hurt to help someone."

She stares at me, her eyes welling with tears, shocked that I would understand.

I say to her formally, "You have honored your mother on this day, daughter of Shyheart. A Ho."

She jumps into my arms, hugging me, "Thank you, Daddy! Thank you!"

"Okay. Are you ready to go meet my sister, the Little Warrior Tree?" I ask, infusing my voice with an upbeat tone to change the energy.

"We're going?" she asks me surprised.

"You're definitely ready!" I confirm.

Her smile, so full of joy and pride, lights up the dark forest.

"You lead. I'm following you," I tell her, showing her the utmost confidence.

We make it to the Little Warrior Tree in twenty minutes, with Angel-Girl leading the way beautifully and as my stepdad, George Allen Cooper, would say, with *style*. The little tree grows out of a crack on top of a lava boulder, which is about ten feet high and nine feet across. We climb up the side and sit down close to the Little Warrior.

I greet her, "A Ho, my sister, this is my daughter, Angel-Girl."

I can see the tree's energy swell up and flow out, welcoming and embracing my daughter. I call this "shining."

Angel-Girl responds brightly, "A Ho, Little Warrior Tree, A Ho!" She is so happy! Then she does exactly the same thing I did the day I met the Little Warrior Tree – she scoots up so both her legs are on either side of the trunk and she wraps her arms around the tree and closes her eyes, leaning her forehead against the bark. It's like two soul sisters meeting. I just let her be, I don't need to give her any guidance. She understands how to honor the Little Warrior. The energy from them merging is shooting out all over the place!

After five minutes, she disengages and slides back so she is sitting next to me. I can see by her shining eyes she connected deeply with my sister. We sit quietly, just feeling "the high-up" as I like to call it. We are at 6000 feet here. The closest person is probably a few miles away. I love this special place!

"Daddy…?" I hear a tentativeness in Angel-Girl's voice. In the last few years, she moves back and forth between "Dad" and "Daddy" and when it's "Daddy" that's a clue to me she really needs my help.

"Yes, my Angel?"

"Is Mommy alone in heaven?" I feel the fear and sadness in her voice.

"Why would you think that, baby?" I say, alarmed.

"Because she doesn't have us." She starts to choke up and crawls over so I can hug her. And in one split second it all makes sense to me. That is really the core of why she is so sensitive to anybody or anything being alone.

"Well, we know she is with God, right?" I feel her nod her head against me. "And, she is with the angels," I add, hoping that helps.

"But she doesn't have us!" she cries.

I go very quiet inside, not reaching for an answer. Then…

"Is that really true, honey?"

"What do you mean?" she asks, sniffling.

"I believe she *feels* us with her. Don't you think?"

"Yeah," she says reluctantly.

"So she *is* with us. She is part of you. You feel her all the time, don't you?"

"Of course, Daddy, she's my mommy."

"Then, haven't you seen that she feels you all the time too. Like today?"

She straightens up and looks at me, as if to say, *Wow I*

didn't think of that. "Mommy and I are…" she interlocks her index finger and thumb from both hands, like she did earlier – meaning *together*.

"Always," I reassure her, softly.

She gives me a big hug. I feel our friend, the wind, start to swirl around us.

"Ready to head down, my Angel?"

"Okay," she says but I can tell she's resistant to go. Lovingly, she reaches out to a branch of the Little Warrior Tree. Something occurs to her and she turns to me, her eyes purposeful again. Then her gaze shifts to her special gold-beaded bracelet. She takes a long moment to absorb its meaning. Silently, she unclasps it and presses it against her heart, closing her eyes to fully take in its power. With great tenderness, Angel-Girl wraps the bracelet around one of the branches of the tree and secures the clasp. "This is for you, Little Warrior Tree," she says with such sweet kindness that it makes my heart swell. "It is very special to me; it represents my mountain lion sister. It will always keep us together. I am here if you need me. Just feel my bracelet and I will feel you. I love you very, very much. Thank you so much for helping my Daddy. A Ho, A Ho."

I stand beside my daughter, fiercely proud of her, in awe of the depth of her caring.

Later that night, after I put Angel-Girl to bed, I head for my bedroom. The energy in the house feels different, very still and wise. I sit down on the end of my bed, just wanting to stay quiet for a moment, but after a few minutes I find myself focusing on my gold ring, rotating it back and forth on my finger. I reflect on the enormous events of the day…*she had your gold ring on*…My bureau, a few feet across from me, pulls my attention. I feel my heart start to pound as I stare at the top drawer. My fingers tap on my special green blanket underneath me, something I do when I am nervous. The drawer pulls me in much the same way I am *pulled* to a sacred location. I must honor its call, as always. I open the drawer and I see what I am looking for, a lapis-blue silk handkerchief tied in a knot. All sorts of feelings run through me: sadness, happiness, being home. That last feeling helps me untie the knot to reveal my Shyheart's gold matching ring. I hold it tight against my heart, closing my eyes, touching that part of me inside that will be never go away, the gratitude for getting to love her.

"Thank you, my love, thank you for coming today." Tears spill on my cheeks. "She said, you have very blue eyes!" I smile. "You definitely do! It's a family thing, right?" I feel our laughter together. I open my hand seeing the ring gleaming up at me. "It's time, right, my girl? It's time." The tears come quicker, nodding my head, knowing this is the moment I have been waiting for. I reach in the drawer and take out the small, felt jewelry box and bring it to my lips and kiss it softly. I open the lid, finding her thin gold-chain necklace. I remember how much Shyheart loved this simple, elegant piece of jewelry. I carefully take it out and open the clasp and thread her ring onto the chain and hold it up to look at it – the lineage. I clutch it against my chest again, feeling its power, feeling my beautiful wife. I head for my little warrior's room. Time has slowed down, and I can feel each step I take. I open her door slowly and see she is sleeping deeply, peacefully, holding Golden-Bear. I move over to her bed as quietly as possible and kneel down next to her. I smile, seeing her dark brown hair is still a tangled mess from our journey, a few tiny leaves we missed sticking out here and there. She is truly a child of the forest. Golden-Bear watches me. I stroke his plush fur, hoping he knows how much I love him, and I put my index finger to my lips to show him I am trying not to wake her. I take the necklace and very gently pick up her head and loop it over her so the ring rests on her tiny hand. I want my daughter to receive this gift while she sleeps so she feels it came directly from her mother. I stand up and gaze down at her. She is her mother's daughter – a determined, gracious, kind warrior.

At the door, I turn and face her, raising my hand in honor and whisper in the language of warriors, "A Ho, Angel-Girl, blood sister to the mountain lion, daughter of Shyheart. Thank you for saving me, thank you, my Angel. A Ho." I place my right hand over my heart and bow softly. I hear the Old Ones singing....

ACKNOWLEDGMENTS

It is important for me to start these acknowledgments in the same way I did for my first book, *The Woodstock Bridge*: the spirit of the Native American Indian has inspired who I am and what I do – this has not changed. I am honored to be called brother by the two Northern Plains Holy Men, who in my mind, raised me. I am with them – that's all there is.

I want to deeply thank Mark Chimsky, my editor and writing coach. He is the embodiment of impeccability. He believed in me and empowered me to take my work to a whole other level. I would also like to thank my literary agent, Marilyn Allen, for her belief in this book; her support has meant so much to me.

I want to thank author and child-protection advocate, Andrew Vachss, who one day "saw" me. His depiction of the Warrior Code resonates through all my work. I hope I have honored him.

Everything I do is in an intimate partnership with the Old Ones, the Grandfather and Grandmother Tree-, Rock-, and Plant-People, Mother Earth, the Great Spirit of the Water, and my brother, the Wind. If I have in some small way honored them with this book, then my mission is complete. The love and support they have shown me is beyond words. It is my deep hope that every page in this book has shown my love and loyalty to them. A Ho, my best friends. Thank you.

To my panther – we are one – my heart is full. Thank you, my special brother, for walking beside me these many years – A Ho.

Throughout the book, you will see mention of A.M.B. (All My Bears). Each day they keep me going, helping me remember the little boy in me because he's the one who "sees." I go, you go – always. This book is my small way of thanking you from the bottom of my heart.

During my stage 4 cancer journey, there was one hero I want to mention and thank with all my heart. I would literally not be alive if it was not for his kindness and belief that he could cure me: Dr. Anthony Berson, radiation oncologist.

I want to especially thank my dear friend, Dr. Candice Perkins, for watching over me and taking such great care of me.

To David Dowd, my business coach of thirty-three years, thanks for the kick in the butt! This book would not have happened without you.

I want to express my love for big G.B. for keeping me safe these past fifteen years.

There are three individuals to whom I want to express my deep gratitude for inspiring me: Bruce Lee for passing on his commitment to "honestly express yourself"; Antonio "El Chocolate" Nunez, considered the greatest of all flamenco singers; and Inia Maxwell, Maori Tribal Leader and Master Haka teacher. These three warriors had a deep influence on me.

In addition, I would like to thank the following friends for supporting me: Bill Minard, Marc Sterling, Pam Clark, Dona Mares, Joe and Michael Bailey, Dicken Bettinger, Mike Niccum, Brian Greenberg, and Glen Paddock, my Jedi master of web design and patience. Also, Anugito ten Voorde for the awesome graphic work and Michael Irvine for letting me use my favorite photograph, *Serendipity*, for the cover.

Finally, to my soul-mate, my thoughts have quieted and what remains are the gifts I was given of deep gratitude and acceptance. I have endeavored to make each single page a gentle prayer as a way of honoring you. I wish all readers the gift she gave me – she understood.

Please Leave A Review On Amazon For
The Shaman & His Daughter!

Also by Gregory Drambour: The Woodstock Bridge

"A Marvelous Adventure! I Recommend It Highly!"
Richard Carlson, author of Don't Sweat The Small Stuff,
NY Times Best-Seller

Native American Spirituality can be a bridge to re-discovering your wisdom! One man's spiritual journey to rediscover the passion and hope he felt in the sixties. His encounter with two warriors from the Sioux Nation, lead him back to his spirit, his wisdom, and the belief that he can still make a difference!

Paperback: $14.95 • ISBN: 0-9719825-1-1
Ebook: $2.95
Available on Amazon, iBook, Barnes & Noble

Author Profile

Gregory Drambour, Master Shamanic Healer, Spiritual Teacher, Author, Owner of Sedona Sacred Journeys

"If you honor them, they will honor you."

A Warrior Spirit lives within each of us! As a stage 4 cancer survivor and with thirty-six years' sobriety, Gregory embraced those powerful words and has been passing them onto thousands of clients in a healing career that has already spanned thirty years. At twenty-eight, Gregory was deeply honored to be taken under the wing of two Northern Plains Holy Men, who passed down to him eleven generations of shamanic knowledge and the warrior code. With that knowledge, Gregory began his life's work of healing and guiding clients on their Sacred Journeys and back to their innate wisdom. His first book, *The Woodstock Bridge*, endorsed by #1 best-selling author Richard Carlson, is considered a must-read for those wanting to go deeper into the world of old-school shamanism and practical spirituality.

For four years in his early forties, Gregory was challenged with stage 4 throat cancer. His success utilizing both alternative and conventional therapies to heal himself has drawn cancer patients and survivors from all over the world to his powerful cellular memory work. Gregory is a passionate advocate and supporter of the National Association to Protect Children and Legislative Drafting Institute for Child Protection, the only two lobbying organizations that exists for children in the United States. He has sat across from an array of clients and seen how their painful childhoods have shaped their adult lives, so he strongly believes that parenting is the key to emotional and spiritual health.

In his teaching and writing, Gregory encourages us to remember that behavior is the truth – this is the code of the warrior. It's not what you do but *how* you do it.

Shaman & His Daughter Site:
http://www.shamanandhisdaughter.com

Gregory Drambour Author Site:
http://www.gregorydrambour.com

Please join me for my online programs, including my shamanic training course

**Shamanic Online Training Program
with Master Shamanic Healer Gregory Drambour**
You will learn Shamanism in the Old Way without the trapping of techniques and new-age rituals. It's about "seeing" with your heart!
http://www.sedonasacredjourneys.com/shamanictraining.htm

Animal Totem Tutorials – 3 Video Tutorials on Developing A Relationship With Your Animal Totem.
http://www.sedonasacredjourneys.com/ALOA/animaltotems.html

Spiritual Warrior Online Training – For Those Wanting To Go Deeper In Their Spirituality.
http://www.sedonasacredjourneys.com/spiritualwarriortraining.html

Social Media & Spiritual Retreat Site
Sedona Sacred Journeys Retreat Organization
http://www.sedonasacredjourneys.com/

Facebook
https://www.facebook.com/sedonasacredjourneys

Instagram
https://www.instagram.com/gregorydrambour/

Twitter
https://twitter.com/GregDrambour

Pinterest
https://www.pinterest.com/GregoryDrambour/

Email: greg@woodstockbridge.com

Made in the USA
San Bernardino, CA
16 August 2019